Elijah

Man of fire, Man of fa

People IN THE BIBLE

John Cheeseman

Day One

First printed 2011

ISBN 978–1–84625–270–9

British Library Cataloguing in Publication Data available

Published by Day One Publications
Ryelands Road, Leominster, HR6 8NZ
☎ 01568 613 740 FAX 01568 611 473
email—sales@dayone.co.uk
web site—www.dayone.co.uk
North American—e-mail—sales@dayonebookstore.com
North American—web site—www.dayonebookstore.com

Cover design by Wayne McMaster
Printed by Orchard Press (Cheltenham) Ltd

This small book shows the author to be a reality-man, a Bible-man, and a God-centred, Christ-exalting and church-loving man. These qualities enable him to see deep into the lessons that Elijah's life has to teach us, and to set them out in a way that searches and strengthens us simultaneously. Cheeseman clears the head, warms the heart and imparts much nourishment by his comments on the story. His book will reward prayerful readers, and will prove ideal for parish study groups.

James I. Packer, Professor of Theology, Regent College, Vancouver, Canada

This is a great little book that will feed the mind and heart. Elijah's story is a key one, with much to teach us, and it needs to be better known and preached about. John makes the helpful and necessary biblical theological connections to the New Testament as a passionate and faithful servant of Christ. I warmly recommend it.

Wallace Benn, Bishop of Lewes, UK

Dedication

To Joy, with all my love

Contents

Throughout my Christian life and ministry, I have been constantly excited and challenged by the life of the prophet Elijah. As we ponder the times in which we live at the beginning of the twenty-first century AD, this man surely speaks to us in a unique and powerful way. Certainly, as far as Great Britain is concerned, we are living in days not dissimilar to those in which Elijah began his public ministry in Israel during the ninth century BC. Things at that time were at a very low ebb, morally and spiritually. Yet, in the providence of God, along came someone who was used wonderfully to challenge the idolatry and ungodliness of the times. Certainly man's extremity was God's opportunity, and it has ever been so.

As we therefore read these stirring Old Testament passages, it will surely be our prayer that God would raise up men like Elijah in our own generation—those who will not be afraid to proclaim the unchanging Word of God.

This book is not an academic treatise. You will not find much here about historical background or Hebrew verbs. If you are interested in those things, I leave you to consult the commentaries. Some may even think that I move too swiftly from the text to practical application, but it is my main desire and purpose to draw attention to those great lessons from the life of the prophet which will challenge and encourage us today in our Christian lives and service. These chapters are based on sermons preached in various contexts over recent years, including the church at Holy Trinity, Eastbourne, where until recently I was the minister.

I would like to thank David and Jean Brooks, members of Holy Trinity, who helped with the typing of the manuscript; also, my wife, Joy, who constantly spurred me on, not only with the writing but also in undertaking a trip to the land of Jordan and Sinai, where I gleaned useful geographical background information.

It is my prayer that the life and work of Elijah will continue to be a great inspiration to us all in these dark and difficult days.

John Cheeseman
Westbrook
Kent

Chapter 1

The darkest hour before the dawn

(1 Kings 16:29–17:1)

In the year 874 BC, Ahab began to reign over Israel (16:29). At this juncture the people of Israel were enduring one of the darkest periods in the whole of their history. Since the death of Solomon in 931 BC, when the kingdom was divided, seven kings had ruled over Israel, and they had all been evil men. The last of these was a man called Ahab, and we are told that he 'did evil in the sight of the LORD, more than all who were before him' (16:30). It is obvious, therefore, that Israel was in a deplorable state. Things could hardly have been worse.

Ahab's attitude to sin

Verse 31 records that Ahab wanted to outdo all his predecessors in wickedness: '... it had been a light thing for him to walk in the sins of Jeroboam'. What exactly were the sins of Jeroboam? The Scriptures record that he made two golden calves and he encouraged the people to worship God under the form of these images (12:28). So he wasn't advocating pagan idolatry, but rather the worship of the true God by means of images, which was a breach of the second commandment rather than the first. However, it was still a gross sin, and it paved the way for Ahab to repudiate altogether the worship of Yahweh.

There are those in the Christian church today who say that it doesn't matter how we worship God so long as we are sincere. If some people find it helpful to have crucifixes around their necks or statues of the Virgin Mary in their buildings, this is deemed acceptable. Against this line of thinking, the Word of God clearly states, 'You shall not make for yourself a carved image' (Exodus 20:4). It does matter how we worship God. Our worship should be governed, not by man-centred impulses or mystical feelings, but by the plain teaching of Holy Scripture.

Notice that it was the beginnings of sin under Jeroboam which led ultimately to the apostasy of Ahab. Having tolerated the worship of the true God by means of images for nearly sixty years, the people eventually lost their sensitivity. They lost their ability to discern truth from error, and so their consciences no longer troubled them when it came to rejecting completely the worship of the true God.

What a sobering lesson this is for us all! Sin is a deadly evil, and we must beware of its beginnings—a little white lie, a little dishonesty, the occasional peep at salacious literature. This is how it all starts, and, before we know it, we are immersed in lust, deceit and corruption. When sin gets a toe in the door, its ultimate intention is to destroy us. Every stirring of envy, if sin had its way, would lead to murder; every doubt concerning the truths of Holy Scriptures would lead to the ultimate denial of God himself; every unclean thought would lead to acts of immorality. Let us make sure that we keep our consciences constantly attuned to the Word of God. If we don't, our consciences will become desensitized, as happened to Ahab, who considered it a 'light thing ... to walk in the sins of Jeroboam' (v. 31).

Ahab's choice of a wife

The next thing we're told about Ahab concerns his marriage to Jezebel. In the second half of 16:31 we read that 'he took for his wife

Jezebel the daughter of Ethbaal king of the Sidonians, and went and served Baal and worshipped him'. In 2 Kings 9:22 we are told that Jezebel was a harlot and a sorceress, and in the book of Revelation 'Jezebel' is the name given to a seductive prophetess who encouraged immorality and idolatry under the cloak of religion (Revelation 2:20). Such a person Ahab decided to marry, and as a consequence he went and served Baal.

It is a sad fact that many a Christian man or woman has been ruined as a result of a distracting relationship with a member of the opposite sex. None of us is immune from this. Even ministers of the gospel have fallen prey to this temptation. It was written of King Solomon that he 'loved many foreign women', and his wives 'turned away his heart' from following the Lord (1 Kings 11:1–3). Let us not be complacent about these things. We can all fall, at any time. It doesn't matter who we are or how long we have been Christians: let us beware of any relationship that is going to draw us away from the things of God.

The nation's attitude to God

In 1 Kings 16:32 we read that Ahab actually set up an altar for Baal in the temple of Baal, which he had built in Samaria. The worship of the true God was formally repudiated and in its place the worship of Baal was established. It now became the official religion of the land. Open defiance of God had reached its climax in Israel. This is made even clearer by what we read in verse 34: 'In his days Hiel of Bethel built Jericho. He laid its foundation at the cost of Abiram his firstborn, and set up its gates at the cost of his youngest son Segub, according to the word of the LORD, which he spoke by Joshua the son of Nun.' What was the significance of this? We read in Joshua 6:26 that Joshua had pronounced a curse, saying that if anyone tried to rebuild Jericho, he would do so with the loss of both his firstborn and his youngest son. Up to this moment in time, no matter how wicked Israel had become, no one had ever dared put God to the test. However, wickedness had so abounded under Ahab that this man, Hiel, actually dared to tempt God. What a terrible state of affairs!

Are there not many parallels here for us today? Do we not live in a day and age when God is being openly repudiated at virtually every level of our national life? He is dragged in only now and again to give the semblance of a little flavour of religion, and so we have the occasional service of celebration or commemoration at St Paul's Cathedral and Westminster Abbey; apart from that, everything is ruled by pure humanism. For all practical purposes, most people live their lives today as if God were dead.

Even those of us who name the name of Christ have become spiritually and morally desensitized to the sickness of our society. We are no longer outraged by such things as easy divorce, abortion on demand, and promiscuity on the television. We accept these things, almost without so much as the bat of an eyelid. Forty years ago, we would have recoiled in horror, but now our consciences hardly twitch. Indeed, there are many within the visible church who are openly advocates of such depravity. Surely a regular reading of Scriptures like Romans 1 will leave us in no doubt about the moral degeneration of our society.

God's provision of a witness

However, all is not lost. After the bad news comes the good news. In the midst of all this darkness and degradation, there suddenly appears on the stage of human history one of the greatest of all the Old Testament prophets. At the beginning of chapter 17, we read these words: 'Now Elijah the Tishbite, of Tishbe in Gilead, said to Ahab, "As the LORD, the God of Israel, lives, before whom I stand, there shall be neither dew nor rain these years, except by my word."' It is fascinating to notice how abruptly Elijah is introduced in the narrative. We are not told how or when he was called by God. It is as if the writer is saying, 'Everything's so desperate here, let's cut through all the preliminaries', and so this whirlwind of a man appears on the scene out of nowhere. What a thrilling moment! As always, God has his man—someone who is not afraid to stand up and be counted for the truth. Elijah was called upon to deliver a most unpalatable message—a message of judgement to the most powerful man in Israel—but because he was conscious that God was with him, he didn't flinch from it. He knew that he was in the presence of God: 'As the LORD, the God of Israel, lives, before whom I stand ...' He could have been writing his own death warrant, but 'If God is for us, who can be against us?' (Romans 8:31). Elijah wasn't going to be pushed around by any human being, not even by the king of Israel.

God never leaves himself without witnesses in this world. Even in the darkest period of human history, he will raise up those like Elijah who will testify that Yahweh is alive in spite of all those who are shouting to the contrary. Are we prepared to be God's witnesses in the days in which we live? Are we prepared to stand up for God in a climate of increasing apostasy? When we are in conversations at work, and the discussion centres on moral and ethical questions, are we prepared to make a stand for Christian principles? Do we shy away from opportunities to witness for Christ because we're afraid of what others might think of us? Or are we going to say, with Elijah, 'As the LORD ... lives, before whom I stand ...'?

Standing up for the true God may mean that we shall experience mockery. It may mean that we don't get promotion at work. For some Christians in the world today, it could even mean death. However, the fear of God is such that it removes from us the fear of man and the fear of consequences. If we are saying, 'No, I can't do that because I'm afraid of the consequences', it shows that we don't fear God enough.

May God grant us the courage and the faith of Elijah. In an age of confusion and compromise, we desperately need men and women who are prepared to stand up and be counted for the truth of the gospel, and who will not yield to the pressures of the world, come what may. Let us follow the example of this great prophet. Do what is right. Commit your way to the Lord—and he will give you the grace to stand firm.

Chapter 2

Lessons at a brook

(1 Kings 17:2–6)

Walking by faith, not by sight

Immediately after Elijah had delivered the message of judgement to Ahab, we read that the word of the Lord came to him with further instructions: 'Depart from here and turn eastward and hide yourself by the brook Cherith' (v. 2). Isn't it interesting to note that Elijah does not receive this fresh guidance until he has first faithfully discharged his commission of speaking to Ahab? This illustrates for us a very important spiritual truth: very often we discover God's will for our lives gradually. Elijah had to go one step at a time. He was not given the whole picture straight away. This is sometimes very difficult to cope with, because, as human beings, we have an insatiable desire to know beyond what God wants us to know. This is what keeps fortune-tellers in business, making thousands of pounds in our 'enlightened' twenty-first century. However, it is not God's way to reveal everything at once. In this world, we must walk by faith, not by sight. God reveals to us only as much as we need to know for present purposes, and we should be content with that.

No doubt Elijah, before leaving to speak to Ahab, would dearly have loved to know what he was supposed to do afterwards, but that was no concern of his for the moment. I think that one of the reasons why we want to know more about the future is the hidden suspicion that perhaps we could alter the situation if we did know. Why do people want to know whether their future husband or wife is going to be good-looking or not so good-looking? Isn't it because they think they might be able to do something about it if they did know? The bottom line is that they are not willing for God to be God; but that is not the Christian way. We need to settle down where God has placed us, and be content to wait patiently for the gradual unfolding of his purposes.

God's ways are not our ways

We don't know much about this place Cherith, but it was obviously somewhere quiet and secluded where the prophet could get away from it all—a place of retreat, where he could recharge his spiritual batteries and prepare for the next stage in his ministry.

How would we have reacted if we had received this command from the Lord at this particular time? Here is the nation in a state of terrible apostasy, and Elijah has just thrown down the gauntlet—'there shall be neither dew nor rain these years, except by my word.' What would we do if we were in Elijah's shoes? Would we not be tempted to go on a tour of all the towns and villages of Samaria, and, as the people see the dew ceasing to fall and wonder why, make the most of this golden opportunity to awaken the conscience of the nation to the things of God? Surely our hearers would be so convicted about the appalling idolatry that they would want to bring pressure upon Ahab to stop it! However, instead of the word of God telling Elijah to go out and call the nation to repentance, the divine instruction was to go and hide away in the wilderness. Verse 4 spells out an even more extraordinary command: 'You shall drink from the brook, and I have commanded the ravens to feed you there.' This is amazing! After all, under the Old Testament law, ravens were categorized as unclean birds. Indeed, in Leviticus 11, they are described as 'detestable' (vv. 13–15); yet here is the Lord using such creatures to feed his prophet!

This illustrates for us the inescapable truth of the Bible, namely, that God's ways are not our ways. If you and I had been in charge of this situation, we would not have told Elijah to bury himself in the middle of nowhere, and then sent ravens to feed him! It doesn't seem to make much sense; but God's mind is not like our minds. As Paul says in Romans 11:33, 'Oh, the depth of the riches and wisdom and knowledge of God! How unsearchable are his judgements and how inscrutable his ways!' We cannot fathom the ways of God. They are mysterious. We should not be surprised by that. After all, we are sinful, finite creatures, and we are trying to grapple with the ways of an almighty, infinite God. It would be surprising if we *could* understand why God does what he does. So let us not get agitated and frustrated when things happen which we can't fathom; remember Elijah and the brook Cherith.

Of course, Elijah was not the first person to have needed a retreat before he began his main public ministry, and he certainly wasn't the last. Moses spent a third of his long life in the desert before God gave him the honour of leading his people out of Egypt. The Lord Jesus spent forty days and forty nights in the wilderness before he began his ministry. The apostle Paul spent some time in the desert region of Arabia before he became the great apostle to the Gentiles. Why was this? Why did God choose to hide away his servant Elijah for this period of time? Could it be that here in the seclusion of Cherith the prophet would be able to learn lessons which would be invaluable for his future ministry? First, there was the lesson of faith. Put yourself in Elijah's situation for a moment. Suppose God told you that ravens were going to come and supply your food. Would you be willing to stake your future existence on a few ravens? You would never have seen ravens do this before. It would be a different matter if God had said to Elijah, 'I'll send down manna from heaven and open up a rock for your water'—at least there would have been a precedent for that. But there was no precedent for ravens. This experience at Cherith would therefore have been a great test of Elijah's faith. Sometimes the Lord will put us in situations in which we simply have to believe God, with no precedent to encourage us. At such times we need to hang on to the sure and certain promises of Scripture as if we are hanging on to a lifeline, always remembering that there is nothing more reliable in all the world than one of God's precious promises.

Depending upon God

The second lesson which Elijah would have learned is that of dependence upon God. There is a sense in which we can be buoyed up by the fellowship of the Lord's people, and that is not wrong. This is why God has placed us in churches; we need one another. But there are times when God cuts us off from all that. In the isolation of a hospital ward, for example, we discover how much or how little we really know of true fellowship with God. In that context we are no longer able to meet with our brothers and sisters in Christ on the Lord's Day, and this becomes a great test of the reality of our walk with God. How much am I depending on him, and how much am I depending on the faith of other Christians?

Notice how the Lord uses both natural and supernatural means to provide for Elijah. On the one hand, there is the natural provision of water from a brook. On the other hand, God commands ravens to bring him food. It is worth pondering the extraordinary providence of the latter. I understand that ravens are greedy creatures who eat anything and everything. Why, then, didn't these ravens eat up the food on their way to Elijah? What a lesson in the absolute sovereignty of God over the forces of nature! God instructs ravens to go against all their natural instincts and bring food to Elijah, without eating it all up en route!

The God of Elijah is the same God we worship today. He is just as able to provide for all our needs today as he was able to provide for the needs of the prophet of old. Usually, he provides for us through ordinary, natural means. On occasions, he does it in more extraordinary ways. However, whether it's ravens or a brook, the fact is that the Lord will provide. That is his sure and certain promise. Jesus says in Matthew 6:33, 'But seek first the kingdom of God and his righteousness, and all these things will be added to you'—and the context of that verse is the provision of material needs. Notice the very important condition attached to this promise—'seek first the kingdom of God'. If we want God to provide for us, we must make sure that we are walking in his ways and obeying his will.

God gave Elijah a specific command to obey: 'Go to the brook Cherith, and there you will find that your needs will be met.' If you are plagued by regular and continual unmet material needs, it is worth asking yourself these questions: Am I living in disobedience to the revealed will of God? Am I in the place of God's appointment—or am I somewhere else?

The blessings of obedience

(1 Kings 17:7–16)

Staying where God has placed us

We read in verse 7 that 'after a while the brook dried up, because there was no rain in the land'. So what was Elijah to do now? Let us again try to put ourselves in the shoes of the prophet. Is it not likely that the devil would have tempted him to think along these lines: 'It's no good staying here. I can't expect to live without anything to drink. Wouldn't it be better to take matters into my own hands and try somewhere else? It might even be better to retrace my steps and risk the vengeance of Ahab than stay here and die of thirst.' However, God had told Elijah to go to Cherith, and he was to stay put until he received further instructions, in spite of the drying brook.

When things start to get difficult in our lives, it is a great temptation to opt out of the situation and move on to something or somewhere else. This happens sometimes to Christians in churches. One or two things start to go wrong. There is a difference of opinion with a fellow-member of the congregation, and so a decision is made to move to another place of worship, without any clear guidance from God that this is the right thing to do. Things are simply beginning to get a bit uncomfortable, so, instead of staying and working through the problem, we choose to leave. We need to recognize that to move out of the will of God is to move out of the place of blessing. The grass may appear to be greener on the other side, but if God hasn't told us to move, we should stay put, because that is where God is going to bless us. Things may be difficult, but that is not the real issue. Can't we trust God to look after us and to work things out for us? Doesn't God know best? We don't have to take matters into our own hands and start doing our own thing. Elijah was commanded to stay by the brook Cherith until he received a fresh word from the Lord to go elsewhere.

The mysteries of God's providence

Eventually the word came. 'Arise, go to Zarephath, which belongs to Sidon, and dwell there. Behold, I have commanded a widow there to feed you' (v. 9). Apparently, Zarephath was some 100 miles away from Cherith, so it was no Sunday afternoon stroll. What is more, it was a difficult journey through the wilderness and mountain passes, and it was to take Elijah right into the very area where Jezebel's father was king. We are told that Zarephath belonged to Sidon, and according to 16:31 the king of the Sidonians was Ethbaal, the father of Jezebel. Yet here is God telling the prophet to take this long and dangerous journey.

Once again, we marvel at the mysteries of God's providence. However much Elijah might have been tempted to doubt the wisdom of this command, we are told in verse 10 that 'he arose and went to Zarephath. And when he came to the gate of the city, behold, a widow was there gathering sticks.'

Before we consider the remarkable obedience of Elijah here to the word of God, let us first consider the great doctrine of God's absolute sovereignty over the affairs of men and women. Just as Elijah was approaching the gate of the city, a widow happened to be there gathering sticks. Is that a strange coincidence? Of course not. The word 'coincidence' does not exist in the language of faith. What to the man or woman of the world is coincidence is, for the child of God, an evidence of God's providence. God so ordered the planning of Elijah's day that at the precise moment he came up to the gates, and not ten minutes beforehand, a widow was there gathering sticks. Our God has control over all the activities of men and women so that here, in this little incident, he brings together the prophet and the widow in the most natural way. The rest of the story goes on to tell us how she responded favourably to Elijah's requests, as a result of which 'she ... and her household ate for many days' (v. 15).

An unbeliever might say that it was fortunate that Elijah should happen to meet such a kind, friendly lady. Elijah could have called upon any number of people who would not have responded so positively; it just so happened that he picked a winner in this widow! But, of course, it didn't 'just so happen'. God had previously told Elijah, 'Behold, I have *commanded* a widow there to feed you' (v. 9, emphasis added). This widow was part and parcel of the sovereign plans and purposes of Almighty God. Almost certainly, she didn't realize this at the time. As far as she was concerned, she was just performing a kindly act for someone who was in need of sustenance after being out in the burning heat of the wilderness. But that didn't matter for the moment. God knew it, and Elijah knew it.

What great confidence it gives us to know that God is absolutely sovereign over all the events of our lives! The God who commanded ravens and widows is the same God we believe in today. Imagine that you take a trip on a train and you pray, 'Lord, move the person to sit next to me that you want, so that I can have the opportunity to witness to him or her about my faith.' Imagine that someone then comes along and sits down, and you get into a conversation about the things of God, and that eventually that person becomes a Christian. Looking back, he or she will say, 'Lord, you commanded me to sit next to that person on the train. I didn't know it at the time, but you did.' Behind what to us appear to be free, natural actions lies the guiding hand of a sovereign God who 'works all things according to the counsel of his will' (Ephesians 1:11). Let us not merely pay lip-service to this great doctrine, but believe it in our hearts as well as our heads. If we do this, it will greatly reduce the strain and the anxiety which torment so many Christians.

In this passage, there are aspects of Elijah's obedience to God's strange command that should be a great challenge to us.

It was immediate

Once the mind of God was known, Elijah sprang into action. Verses 8–9 say, 'Then the word of the LORD came to him, "Arise, go to Zarephath ..."' Verse 10 says, 'So he arose and went ...' There is no evidence of any hesitation or delay.

Anything less than immediate obedience is really disobedience. In Psalm 119:59–60, we read,

> When I think on my ways,
> I turn my feet to your testimonies.
> I hasten and do not delay
> to keep your commandments.

How do we react when the Lord speaks to us through his Word, perhaps pointing out some sin that needs to be rooted out of our lives? Do we not often respond along these lines: 'Lord, I thank you for speaking to me in this way. I realize that this is your word to me, but I'm not going to deal with it just at the moment. There are circumstances that keep me from obeying it immediately. Some other time Lord.' The problem is this: if we don't obey immediately, the conscience, by degrees, becomes insensitive, and in the end we almost forget what God originally said. I am reminded of Augustine, who, when he was keeping a concubine and his conscience terrified him, prayed, 'Lord, deliver me from this terrible sin, but not now.' Elijah's obedience was immediate.

It was unquestioning

In spite of the strangeness of the command, there is no evidence that Elijah argued with God about it. He simply packed his bags and did as he was told. Why was this? Surely because he had confidence in the One who was giving the command. After all, he had already proved God to be faithful to his word at Cherith. That had been another peculiar instruction, yet God had not let him down but had sent ravens to feed him in the wilderness. So why shouldn't God be trusted in this new situation?

Often, when the path of obedience is marked out for us and we see that it involves difficulties, instead of focusing our minds upon the character of the God who has marked out the path, we say things like: 'Why that path? It doesn't seem fair. It's going to be difficult.' Elijah, on the other hand, gave unquestioning obedience because, rather than filling his mind with the problems of the journey ahead, he looked up to heaven and said, 'Who is the God who commands me? Is he not the God of love, the God of tender concern for his children and the God of power? Therefore, as I walk in that path, I know he will look after me.' Elijah was preoccupied with the God who marked out the path, not with the difficulty of the path itself. There is all the difference in the world between these two positions.

If we want to give unquestioning obedience to the Word of God, we need to fill our minds with thoughts of God's character. Is he not the God who has redeemed us in Christ? Are not even the hairs of our head all numbered in his sight? Is he not the one before whom not a sparrow falls to the ground without his concern?

It was complete

Elijah didn't get three-quarters of the way to Zarephath and then get cold feet. No, he kept right on to the end of the road, unlike so many Christians today who give up at the slightest hint of trouble. Just as delayed obedience is disobedience, so too is partial obedience. For example, if God tells us to do six things and we do five, we would probably think we have done pretty well. But that is not the way God sees it, because it is the neglect of that sixth thing which reveals the true state of our hearts. Here is the real test of Christian discipleship: Am I prepared to obey God, even when it hurts?

It was this kind of complete obedience which the Lord Jesus gave to God the Father, and at times it cost him dearly. In Gethsemane, for example, it cost him sweat-drops of blood. If you are a Christian, it won't be long before you face some personal Gethsemanes. There will be times when to render complete obedience to the will of God will cost you dearly. It may, for example, cost you close friends and even relatives. This is why Jesus said, 'Whoever loves father or mother more than me is not worthy of me, and whoever loves son or daughter more than me is not worthy of me' (Matthew 10:37). If there is a choice between a parent or Christ, the parent's wish, no matter how earnest, must be rejected. If the choice is between a child or Christ, the child's wish, no matter how appealing, must be overruled. Like Elijah, our obedience needs to be immediate, unquestioning and complete.

You may be thinking, 'Is it really worth it—all this blood, sweat and tears? Are not the demands of the Christian life too great? Is it not too hard?' Let me therefore conclude this chapter on a positive note! Although the Christian life can be very costly at times, the way of obedience is the way of God's richest blessing. We see this principle wonderfully illustrated in our passage. Although it was a mighty strange command for the prophet to go to Zarephath, what did he find when he arrived there? God had commanded a widow to provide for his physical needs.

This is the constant theme of the Bible. Obedience leads to blessing. If we put God first and obey his commands, he won't let us down. God is no man's debtor. If, on the other hand, we look first to our own self-interest, the result will be disappointment, frustration and disillusionment. Jesus said, 'For whoever would save his life will lose it, but whoever loses his life for my sake will find it' (Matthew 16:25).

Is the Christian life worth it? Absolutely!

Chapter 4

The secret of effective prayer

(1 Kings 17:17–24)

From sunshine to clouds

The passage studied in the previous chapter ended on a very happy note. God wonderfully provided for the needs of the prophet, not to mention those of the widow and her son. 'And she and he and her household ate for many days. The jar of flour was not spent, neither did the jug of oil become empty ...' In the midst of a terrible famine, the widow and her son were saved by Elijah from destitution, and everything in the garden seemed to be rosy.

However, we then move into verse 17, and immediately the whole situation changes: 'After this the son of the woman, the mistress of the house, became ill. And his illness was so severe that there was no breath left in him.' In this situation of sunshine and happiness we are suddenly introduced to the dark providence of death.

There will undoubtedly be occasions in our lives when we have to face dark providences of one kind or another—when a sunny day becomes a cloudy day, and the smile of God becomes hidden from us behind some terrible tragedy. God never promised us that it would be sunshine all the way. 'In the world you will have tribulation,' said Jesus (John 16:33), and sometimes troubles come upon us very suddenly and very unexpectedly, as in the case of the widow here. One moment everything seems to be going marvellously well, with the presence of a prophet of God and an unfailing supply of food, and the next moment her son becomes so desperately ill that he dies.

Why does God allow such things to happen? Why did God make sure that this widow had enough food for herself and her son, and then the next moment allow her son to die? On the surface, it doesn't make any sense. However, with the benefit of hindsight, we can see that, through this experience of darkness, the widow came face to face with the power of Almighty God (see v. 24), and the prophet Elijah learned important lessons about prayer which would be invaluable to him when later he confronted the prophets of Baal on Mount Carmel. There is always a purpose in suffering. God uses it to teach us lessons about himself which we would otherwise not learn in happier, sunnier days.

Lessons learned about prayer

In this passage we see a classic case of effective prayer in a crisis. And what a crisis it was: the death of a little boy. In Old Testament history, there was no precedent of God raising someone from physical death to life. Yet we read in verse 19 that, calmly and confidently, Elijah said to the woman, 'Give me your son', and then took him upstairs, laid him on the bed and prayed. How could the prophet remain so cool in such a crisis? What a contrast to the widow! She was nearly beside herself: 'What have you against me, O man of God? You have come to me to bring my sin to remembrance and to cause the death of my son!' Isn't that typical of the way so many people react in a crisis? They become bitter, and they start pointing the finger of accusation at others. Not so Elijah. Instead of panicking, he confidently laid the situation before the Lord in prayer. What was the secret?

A cultivated prayer life

Surely part of the answer is that this was not the first time Elijah had ever prayed. He was a man who constantly lived in the presence of God. Remember that he had said to Ahab, at the beginning of chapter 17, 'As the LORD, the God of Israel, lives, *before whom I stand...*' (emphasis added). That was the basic attitude of his life; he lived before the eye of God. No doubt he also learned vital lessons about communion with God when he was alone by the brook Cherith for a period of time. Elijah already had such a familiarity with the throne of grace that, when the crisis came in verse 17, it wasn't at all unnatural for him to pray boldly and fervently.

Prayer, like all the other graces of the Christian life, is something that is cultivated and developed through use. The opposite is also true: it shrivels and decays when neglected. The way that we react in a crisis speaks volumes about our prayer lives. If we go to pieces, as this woman did, it suggests very strongly that we spend far too little time in prayer. If, on the other hand, we want to be those who will pray effectively in a future crisis, we need to start becoming disciplined about our times of prayer here and now. We can only explain the remarkable praying of Elijah in verses 20 and 21 by seeing it in the overall context of a life of regular and constant communion with God.

Compassion for others

In addition, it is obvious that Elijah was filled with a holy love and compassion for this widow and her son. After all, she had just been very rude and aggressive towards him in verse 18. Yet, despite these unjust accusations, he said to her in verse 19, 'Give me your son.' He gladly took to heart the needs of others; and if we are to be effective men and women of prayer, our hearts must likewise be full of love and compassion towards those in need. Would Elijah have prayed any more boldly and fervently if this had been his own son? When we read about the intensity of his praying in verse 21, it is hard to believe that he would. How long has it been since we took to heart someone else's need just as deeply as if it had been our own? How long has it been since we prayed to God for the sick relative of a friend just as fervently as if we were praying for one of our own relatives?

A focus on the covenant-keeping God

What was the basis of Elijah's prayer in this passage? In verse 20 we read that he cried to the Lord, saying, 'O LORD my God.' Then 'he stretched himself upon the child ... and cried, "O LORD my God."' The word translated 'LORD' is the Hebrew word 'Yahweh', which was the special covenant name for God. Elijah had a constant awareness of God as a faithful covenant-keeping God—and a covenant-keeping God not only to his people in general, but also to him in particular: 'my God'. 'I am in covenant with you,' says the prophet. 'I am yours, and you are mine.' So the first thing that Elijah did when he prayed was to bring into focus who God was, and his relationship to such a God.

One of the great weaknesses of our praying is the fact that, too often, we don't take time to get our minds into that kind of focus. The result is that we pray weakly, and we ask meagrely, because we don't really believe that God is our loving heavenly Father who longs to bless us because we are his children. If we are to be really effective in prayer, we must bring this thought before us, not only as we begin to pray, but also throughout our praying. This is why Elijah restated the expression 'O LORD my God' in verse 21—not in vain repetition, but because he was constantly aware of the One to whom he was making his request—'Yahweh, my God'.

The spirit of Elijah's prayer

IT WAS INTENSE

We read in verse 20 that 'he cried to the LORD', and then in verse 21, 'he stretched himself upon the child three times' and again 'cried to the LORD'. We get the picture of a man who was engaged in what he was doing with every cell of his being. I confess to my shame that I know very little of this kind of intense praying, but what little I do know leads me to conclude that it is one of the most demanding things in the whole of the Christian life. It requires total effort and total concentration, with absolutely no distractions.

IT WAS INTELLIGENT

Notice how he reasons with God in verse 20: 'O LORD my God, have you brought calamity even upon the widow with whom I sojourn, by killing her son?' In effect he is saying, 'Lord, this is a widow, and you've revealed in your Word that you have a special concern for widows. Moreover, this is the widow with whom I am staying. She is the one who has shown kindness to me. Surely you are the God who rewards such people! What kind of reward is this—to kill her only son? Furthermore, what about your name and character? This poor widow has only just begun to understand something of your ways. What will this look like in her eyes?'

Elijah is intelligently bringing before God in prayer what the old writers used to call 'divine argument'. He is giving specific reasons why he believes that God should intervene in this situation. This is a perfectly legitimate thing to do. God wants us to use our minds when we pray. This is why Paul says in 1 Corinthians 14, 'I will pray with my spirit, but I will pray with my mind also' (v. 15). It is quite in order for us to bring before God reasons why we believe he should act—always, of course, with the recognition that we may not be viewing the reasons rightly, and always with the attitude 'not my will, but yours be done'.

IT WAS PERSISTENT

We are told in verse 21 that he stretched himself upon the boy three times as he cried to the Lord. What would have happened if Elijah had stretched himself only twice and cried to the Lord? I guess that, from the human standpoint, we would have to say that Elijah's prayer would not have been answered, because he did not persist. Time and time again the Bible emphasizes the need for persistent, persevering prayer. Jesus said, 'Ask, and it will be given to you; seek, and you will find; knock, and it will be opened to you' (Matthew 7:7). The Greek verbs in that text are present imperatives, which have the force of 'go on asking; go on seeking; go on knocking'. In other words, don't give up at the first hurdle. Keep on keeping on. Many of us, if we're honest, would have to admit that often we give up before the desired blessing comes. Perhaps the reason we do so is because we don't want to carry on praying for something that it is not God's will to grant.

I would suggest, however, that there is *every reason* for us to persist in prayer, unless and until the Lord brings some new light on the situation that leads us to change the way that we are praying. Let us not quit simply because it is the third, fourth or even fiftieth time of asking. As long as there are still reasons why we believe God ought to work in the light of his Word, we should surely persist with a holy persistence and not give up.

Chapter 5

Darkness and light

(1 Kings 18:1–17)

At the beginning of 1 Kings 18, Elijah gets his marching orders once again: 'Go, show yourself to Ahab' (v. 1). In 1 Kings 17 we saw two commands from the Lord to his prophet—first to go to Cherith, and then to go to Zarephath, both of them unlikely places. But now the time has come for the big showdown. God tells Elijah to go and meet his mortal enemy—the man who, given half a chance, would kill him, along with all the other prophets who had already come to a sticky end (see 18:4).

What was the reason for this fresh command? The second half of verse 1 gives us the answer: 'I will send rain upon the earth,' says the Lord. We remember from 17:1 that Elijah had already made it clear to Ahab that 'there shall be neither dew nor rain these years, except by my word'. So now the time has come for the drought to end, and God wants Ahab to know that this is no accident. It's not going to rain because of prayers to Baal. No; it's going to rain because God says so through his prophet.

How does Elijah respond to this new command? In the same way he responded to the first two commands. We read in verse 2 that he 'went to show himself to Ahab'. That is a very simple, short statement, but consider the implications. Here is God telling the prophet to go and stand before his most implacable enemy, yet Elijah does it without any argument. I am reminded of Paul in Acts 20:24, when he said, 'I do not account my life of any value nor as precious to myself, if only I may finish my course and the ministry that I received from the Lord Jesus.'

'I don't look upon my life', says Paul, 'as a precious jewel to be preserved in a casket, but rather as capital to be spent in the cause of Jesus Christ.' The whole concept of self-preservation is entirely foreign to the spirit of biblical Christianity. If the command of God leads us to the jaws of death, we should say, 'So be it! To the jaws we go!'

There is a major contrast between two of the principal characters in this section. On the one hand, there is Ahab, who is a terrible warning to us of the sinfulness of sin in the human heart. On the other hand, there is Obadiah, who is a striking example of practical godliness.

Ahab

HIS ATTITUDE TO GOD'S PROPHETS

We read in verse 4 that Ahab allowed his wife, Jezebel, to murder all the prophets except for the 100 rescued by Obadiah. Then, when Ahab came face to face with Elijah himself in verse 17, he asked, 'Is it you, you troubler of Israel?' showing no respect whatsoever for the person and mission of God's prophet.

A man's attitude towards a prophet of God is a sure indication of his attitude towards God himself. Indeed, the Lord Jesus said as much in Matthew 10:40, when he sent out the twelve apostles to preach the word: 'Whoever receives you receives me, and whoever receives me receives him who sent me.' A good question for us to ask ourselves, therefore, is this: What is my attitude to the Word of God, whether preached or read? Am I like Ahab, thinking, 'I wish God would leave me alone'? Or do I have the attitude, 'Speak, LORD, for your servant hears' (1 Samuel 3:9)? One of the best barometers of our spiritual condition is our attitude to the Word of God. If our souls are in a healthy state, we will delight to hear the Word of God, even if it stabs our consciences.

HIS ATTITUDE TO GOD'S JUDGEMENTS

Ahab doesn't see any connection between the terrible famine and his own sin. So, when he meets Elijah, he says, in effect, 'You're the one who's causing all this trouble, not me!' What appalling cheek and hypocrisy! It was the king's evil influence in Israel that had led to the famine, and yet here he is, shifting the blame onto somebody else. Isn't that typical of the sinfulness of the human heart? It started back in the Garden of Eden, when Adam said to God, 'The woman whom you gave to be with me, she gave me fruit of the tree, and I ate' (Genesis 3:12). 'It's not my fault, Lord; it's this wretched woman who's caused all the trouble!' We rarely admit that something is our own fault. If you're a husband and things are going wrong in the family, you blame your wife. If you're a wife, you blame your husband. Or perhaps you blame it on the children—they're the cause of all the trouble. Does it never occur to us that some of the problems might lie within ourselves and result from the fact that we are unwilling to allow the Word of God to expose our own sinfulness? May God deliver us from this spirit of constantly shifting the blame elsewhere.

HIS ATTITUDE TOWARDS HIS SUBJECTS

Next to the glory of God, Ahab's first concern in the midst of all this famine and desolation should have been those over whom he ruled as king. But what was he really concerned about? We read in verse 5 that he said to Obadiah, 'Go through the land to all the springs of water and to all the valleys. Perhaps we may find grass and save the horses and mules alive.' How incredible! Mothers and little children are dying of starvation. The whole land is under the curse of God, and all Ahab is bothered about is finding grass for his animals! What a further revelation of the corruption that is possible in the human heart!

What are our priorities as Christians? Are our chief concerns the glory of God and the welfare of others, or looking after our own selfish interests? We may have heard the children's talk on 'JOY'—Jesus first, Others second, Yourself last—but how many of us actually live out that principle in our daily lives? If we are honest, we are wrapped up with sin and self much of the time.

Obadiah

On a much more positive note, let us consider the example of Obadiah. Here we move out of the darkness into the light, because we are told at the end of verse 3 that he 'feared the LORD greatly'. This is quite remarkable when we consider the circumstances of Obadiah's life. He was a steward in charge of the king's household (v. 3), which meant that he was exposed to all the idolatry of Ahab and Jezebel. Yet, in spite of all these ungodly influences, he maintained a holy reverence for the God of Israel. What a shining example to us today, as we seek to live for Christ in a world of similar godlessness and immorality.

HIS ATTITUDE TO GOD

What exactly does the text mean when it says that 'Obadiah feared the LORD greatly'? Surely it means that he had a devout respect for the person and the character of God—a recognition of God's majesty and holiness, and a realization of his own unworthiness in God's presence. Because Obadiah had that kind of respect, he sought to please God and obey his commandments. Amid all the wickedness of Ahab's court, and all the king's aggressive attempts to blot out true religion in the land, Obadiah said to himself, 'I must conduct my life in a way that brings honour to the God whom I worship.' There was always something that mattered more than the frowns of Ahab and Jezebel. It was this: 'What will my God say? What will please or displease him?'

There is a striking example of this principle being put into action in verse 16. When Elijah tells Obadiah in verse 8 to announce his arrival to Ahab, Obadiah hesitates and he says, in effect, 'If I do that, Ahab will kill me' (vv. 9–14). But when Elijah repeats the instruction in verse 15 with the words, 'As the LORD of hosts lives', Obadiah springs into action (v. 16). Why the contrast? Surely it is because Obadiah now realizes that what the prophet says is bound by the word and character of Almighty God himself. Elijah is not speaking 'off the cuff'. Here is a word of divine authority, and in response, Obadiah goes off to meet the king straight away.

HIS ATTITUDE TO GOD'S PROPHETS

We have already noted Ahab's terrible attitude towards God's prophets. What a striking contrast we see here in the life of Obadiah! We read in verse 4 that 'when Jezebel cut off the prophets of the LORD, Obadiah took a hundred prophets and hid them by fifties in a cave and fed them with bread and water'. When Obadiah met Elijah, he 'fell on his face and said, "Is it you, my Lord Elijah?"' (v. 7). Obadiah showed great respect for the prophet of God, in contrast with the rude and aggressive attitude of Ahab in verse 17.

We don't have any prophets like Elijah today, but we do have the complete revelation of God in Holy Scripture. The lesson for us today, therefore, is this: let us not speak of loving and fearing God unless we are prepared to sit under the authority of his Word. It is sheer folly and delusion for us to think that we are living godly lives if we are not submitting ourselves to the teaching of the Bible.

HIS GODLY UPBRINGING

In verse 12, Obadiah testifies to the fact that he has feared the Lord *from his youth*. Indeed, his very name indicates a godly upbringing: 'Obadiah' literally means 'servant of Yahweh'. In the midst of all this apostasy in Israel, there were parents who wanted it to be known to their contemporaries, many of whom were Baal worshippers, that they were not happy with such idolatry. The very name of their son would be an arrow in the consciences of their pagan neighbours.

We cannot overestimate the importance of a godly upbringing, especially in days of apostasy such as our own. It is possible to bring up children in the fear of the Lord even in the darkest periods of human history; Obadiah was living proof of that. If you have children, what is your greatest ambition for them? Is it that they get good educational qualifications and make a lot of money? Or is it that they grow up, like Obadiah, to be servants of the living God? And if the latter is indeed your greatest desire, do you let them know that? It is one thing to have that ambition hidden away in your heart, but Obadiah's parents weren't content with that. They actually stuck it on his name! They made it quite clear what they wanted for him.

What a wonderful example and inspiration Obadiah is for us today! Many of us live and work in a court of Ahab, with all the cursing, foul language, idolatry and immorality. Yet Obadiah stands as a testimony to the fact that it is possible to live as a righteous person, even in the presence of the worst of the ungodly. The important challenge that comes down to us across the centuries is this: Are we acting as salt and light in the various situations in which God has placed us? Or has the salt lost its taste? Are we guilty of compromise with sin? May God grant that in our generation we may live as Obadiah did, fearing the Lord greatly, and demonstrating by life and practice the reality of true godliness.

Who is on the Lord's side?

(1 Kings 18:18–24)

A passion for the truth

In response to Ahab's hypocritical question in 1 Kings 18:17, Elijah replies with the most extraordinary candour and boldness: 'I have not troubled Israel, but you have, and your father's house, because you have abandoned the commandments of the LORD and followed the Baals' (v. 18). There is no attempt here to pacify the king. There is no cowering before the might of Ahab and his court. Instead, Elijah makes it painfully clear that all the terrible devastation and ruin in Israel is the fault of one man, and that man is certainly not himself!

How could the prophet be so honest and fearless in the face of this wicked and dangerous man? Surely because of his love of the truth. Above all other things, Elijah was consumed with a passion that the name of God be vindicated in the midst of a Baal-worshipping community. As he stood before Ahab, he wanted the king to know why the nation was in its current state, and if that meant putting his own life on the line in the process, so be it.

We will never become Elijahs in our generation until our love of God's truth becomes more important to us than love of our own lives and reputations. Why are we so often silent in our Christian witness? Is it not because we love our reputations too much? Elijah didn't care what Ahab thought of him. All he was concerned about was that Ahab should know the truth about himself. The great Scottish preacher Robert Murray McCheyne once said, 'The man who loves you most is the man who tells you the most truth about yourself.' Do we love the souls of men and women enough that we are prepared to be honest with them? Are we willing to be considered an enemy in order to be a true friend to someone? Isn't this what Paul was talking about in Galatians 4:16, when he said, 'Have I then become your enemy by telling you the truth?'

The sovereignty of God

Elijah's boldness continues in verse 19, when he says, 'Now therefore send and gather all Israel to me at Mount Carmel.' This is an astonishing scenario. Here is the prophet not merely charging the king with his crimes, but actually giving him orders! And what is more, Ahab meekly does as he's told, because we read in verse 20 that he 'sent to all the people of Israel and gathered the prophets together at Mount Carmel'. The only explanation for this extraordinary state of affairs, in which the king has become an errand-boy to the prophet, is found in the great truth of Proverbs 21:1: 'The king's heart is a stream of water in the hand of the LORD; he turns it wherever he will.' Once again, we have to marvel at the great doctrine of the absolute sovereignty of God over the affairs of men and women. If we are Christians, we can sleep peacefully in our beds at night, knowing that the present-day Ahabs are in the hands of God and can do nothing without his say-so.

Sitting on the fence

We read in verse 21 that Elijah 'came near to all the people'—one man, standing against a nation, a king and 850 false prophets—and he threw out a question that must have pierced them all to the heart: 'How long will you go limping between two different opinions? If the LORD is God, follow him; but if Baal, then follow him.' In other words, 'It's about time you people had the courage of your convictions! If God really is God, then follow him. If he really is the supreme governor of the universe, then he deserves your undivided allegiance. Commit yourself to his ways, whatever the cost. On the other hand, if you owe your existence and salvation to Baal, then give him what he deserves. Stop tottering like a drunken man between the two! Make up your minds, once and for all!'

How did the people respond to this challenge? We read that they 'did not answer him a word' (v. 21). There was absolute silence. They didn't know what to say because they enjoyed sitting on the fence. On the one hand, they weren't absolutely convinced that Baal was God. On the other hand, they weren't prepared to give the true God their unreserved allegiance and service. In that respect, they were like so many people in our world today.

There is nothing more abhorrent to God than indecision in religious commitment. Jesus says in Matthew 6:24, 'No one can serve two masters, for either he will hate the one and love the other, or he will be devoted to the one and despise the other.' There is no room for compromise when it comes to the things of God. In a similar vein, the risen Saviour says these startling words in Revelation 3:15–16: 'I know your works: you are neither cold nor hot. Would that you were either cold or hot! So, because you are lukewarm, and neither hot nor cold, I will spit you out of my mouth.'

If we are honest, many of us are guilty of this double-mindedness in spiritual matters. We would like to think that we follow the true God alone. After all, we would never be found worshipping in a pagan temple! That would be unthinkable. We go to church every Sunday, and we lift up our voices to the true and living God. But what about the rest of the week? Do we allow the Word of God to govern our lives from Monday to Saturday—in our business ethics, our relationships in the home, our words on the telephone, how we spend our time and what we choose to watch on television? Jesus wants to be Lord of everything in our lives. There is no area that is off-limits to the eternal Son of God. Where do we stand on this? Are we like the people of Israel, who wanted to 'limp between two different opinions'?

Playing the numbers game

Having delivered the great challenge of verse 21, Elijah says to the people, 'I, even I only, am left a prophet of the LORD, but Baal's prophets are 450 men' (v. 22). Elijah is not suggesting that he is the only true worshipper of God in the land; he is saying that he is the *only true prophet* left. But what about the 100 prophets whom Obadiah had hidden in verse 4? Were they not still alive? If they were, they were apparently too afraid to show their faces in public. There is absolutely no hint that they were present on Mount Carmel. So, as far as Elijah was concerned, he was the only prophet who was prepared publicly to nail his colours to the mast. Everyone else had been silenced. Just one man was left standing alone.

In times of spiritual darkness, true prophets of God are always in the minority. However, truth can never be decided by the counting of heads. If the numbers game was being played on Mount Carmel, Baal would have won hands down. After all, could one person possibly be right, and 450 people be wrong? Elijah was outnumbered and outvoted. But numbers in themselves prove nothing. Just because Christians are in the minority, it doesn't mean that we are wrong. Jesus said, 'For the gate is wide and the way is easy that leads to destruction, and those who enter by it are many. For the gate is narrow and the way is hard that leads to life, and those who find it are few' (Matthew 7:13–14).

There is a great temptation for the Christian church today to play the numbers game. For example, if we become desperate for outward success, we can easily soft-pedal those aspects of the gospel message that are offensive to the natural man, such as the teaching on hell and judgement, or the need for repentance and the cost of discipleship. 'Let's leave these things out in case we put people off' is the philosophy in many churches. However, Christian conversion is not a work of man. It is a work of the Holy Spirit. We must therefore boldly declare 'the whole counsel of God' (Acts 20:27) and leave the results in his hands.

Seeking signs and wonders

Before we conclude this chapter, let us consider the actual test which Elijah proposed to the false prophets:

> 'Let two bulls be given to us, and let them choose one bull for themselves and cut it in pieces and lay it on the wood, but put no fire to it. And I will prepare the other bull and lay it on the wood and put no fire to it. And you call upon the name of your god, and I will call upon the name of the LORD, and the God who answers by fire, he is God.' And all the people answered, 'It is well spoken.'

It is fascinating to contrast the people's response in verse 24 with their earlier response in verse 21. When presented with a spiritual challenge to their hearts and consciences, they didn't want to know. But now that they were presented with the possibility of witnessing a miracle, they were very interested! However, a desire for miracles, coupled with an unwillingness to face moral issues, is an evidence of spiritual barrenness and immaturity. We find exactly the same kind of mentality in our Lord's own day. The scribes and Pharisees said to

Jesus, '"Teacher, we wish to see a sign from you." But he answered them, "An evil and adulterous generation seeks for a sign"' (Matthew 12:38–39).

There are those in the church today who are pressing for signs and wonders. They say that if only the gospel could be authenticated by miracles, folk would be converted to Christ in large numbers. But is this really the case? After all, when the people of Israel were wandering through the wilderness after the exodus, God fed them every day with supernatural manna from heaven. Did this result in great spiritual blessing? Not at all. We are told that, because of their sinfulness and unbelief, God allowed them to die in the wilderness, and he had to raise up a whole new generation to enter the promised land. Signs and wonders have no inherent power to change the hearts of men and women, which is why Abraham said to the rich man in Luke 16:31, 'If they do not hear Moses and the Prophets, neither will they be convinced if someone should rise from the dead.' If people will not be persuaded by the truths of the Word of God, witnessing miracles won't make any difference to them. In this connection, it is interesting to note that, although the people did make an initial response of faith in 1 Kings 18:39, as we shall see later, this proved to be superficial, and they soon relapsed into idolatry.

The folly of false religion

(1 Kings 18:25–29)

Divine mockery

The great contest between the prophets of Baal and the true God of Israel is about to reach its dramatic climax on Mount Carmel. We read in 1 Kings 18:25 that Elijah allowed the false prophets to choose for themselves one of the two available bulls, so that there could be no accusation of any unfairness. They were then to make all the necessary preparations for the sacrifice, with one important restriction: no fire was to be put to the wood, so as to prevent the possibility of fraud. They were forced to rely upon a direct appeal to their deity, which they proceeded to give from morning till noon. For three solid hours, they called upon their god, saying, 'O Baal, answer us!' But, in spite of this ceaseless chanting, we are told that 'there was no voice, and no one answered' (v. 26).

It has been pointed out that Satan could have sent fire down upon this offering, had God allowed him to do so. After all, the devil is quite capable of performing signs and wonders; think of the magicians in Egypt. However, on this particular occasion, God did not allow Satan to use his power because this was a public contest between Yahweh and Baal, and the Lord wanted to vindicate his name in the sight of all the people.

What were the prophets going to do in the face of this deafening silence? Their prayers had proved to be useless. We read in verse 26 that they decided to leap around the altar. They probably reasoned to themselves, 'Our god is not going to be moved by plain words; we need to give him something of the activity of our bodies.' While all this was going on, Elijah mocked them, saying, 'Cry aloud, for he is a god. Either he is musing, or he is relieving himself, or he is on a journey, or perhaps he is asleep and must be awakened.' We might be shocked by this sarcasm, but there is such a thing as divine mockery in Scripture. In Psalm 2, we are told that God laughs and holds in derision those who take counsel against the Lord and his Anointed (v. 4). There is a place for mockery when that to which people have given themselves is absolutely foolish and irrational.

How did the prophets of Baal respond to all this? Here we come to one of the most pathetic parts of the whole narrative. Instead of acknowledging their stupidity, they raised their feverish activity to an even higher pitch: 'they cried aloud and cut themselves after their custom with swords and lances, until the blood gushed out upon them. And as midday passed, they raved on until the time of the offering of the oblation ...' (vv. 28–29). Apparently, this offering was made at three o'clock in the afternoon, so for another three hours these foolish, deluded prophets kept on with their wailing and chanting and mutilating their bodies. But it was all in vain. We read at the end of verse 29 that there was still no voice. 'No one answered; no one paid attention.' Baal worship was exposed for all to see as a complete sham.

What does all this have to say to us today?

The folly of idol worship

In the first place, it shows us the absolute folly of giving allegiance to anything or anyone other than the true and living God. Do we have idols in our lives? What about love of money? The desire to keep up with the Joneses can become all-absorbing. Or what about pleasure?

Do we put the things we enjoy before the service of God? Even for Christians, a television programme can become more important than Sunday worship.

Perhaps our idol is status and position, like the Pharisees who wanted the best seats in the synagogues. We love other people to look up to us. We so much want to be in the public eye, getting all the attention. Yet Jesus said, '... the last will be first, and the first last' (Matthew 20: 16). Or what about our work? Could that be our Baal? Some Christians become so obsessed with their jobs that they can think of little else, and work becomes a modern form of Baal worship.

The folly of pagan prayer

A second warning from this passage concerns the folly of pagan concepts of prayer. Six solid hours of chanting, dancing and self-mutilation was part of their concept of calling upon their deity. Why did they imagine that all this would somehow help in getting an answer? It was because they considered these gods to be reluctant and tight-fisted, and such reluctance needed to be overcome by long prayers and all kinds of external rituals and paraphernalia. This is what Jesus was talking about in the Sermon on the Mount when he said, 'And when you pray, do not heap up empty phrases as the Gentiles do, for they think that they will be heard for their many words' (Matthew 6:7). In other words, the heathen look upon their deity as a being who is reluctant and unconcerned, and therefore a large number of long petitions are necessary in order to get any results. Let us not misunderstand this point: our Lord is not condemning long prayers as such. If this were a blanket condemnation of lengthy prayers, we would have to write off many of the prayers that we find recorded in Holy Scripture. What Jesus is primarily concerned about is our motive in prayer. Pagans pray on and on and on, because they imagine that the longer and louder they pray, the greater will be their chance of success. This is a completely unbiblical concept. The acceptability of our prayers does not depend upon the number of words we use or upon the number of prayers we rattle off.

Sometimes, however, we can be guilty of similar attitudes. We can pray as though we don't really believe that God's heart is open towards us in love and grace. We can think that we somehow need to twist God's reluctant arm for him to give us a blessing. Yes, of course we need to be persistent and persevering in prayer, as we saw from Chapter 4, but that doesn't mean that God is unwilling to respond to us. Jesus says in Matthew 7:11, 'If you then, who are evil, know how to give good gifts to your children, how much more will your Father who is in heaven give good things to those who ask him!' Our God is in no way reluctant to bless us.

Let me extend the application further. Some Christians have the mistaken idea that not much has been accomplished in prayer because they have not risen to a certain level of emotional involvement. They don't experience a great emotional feeling, so they think that God hasn't really heard their prayers. However, such an understanding of prayer owes more to paganism than Christianity. The measure of our feelings and emotions has nothing whatever to do with God's faithfulness and willingness to answer our prayers; what matters is that we come into the presence of God with clean hands and a pure heart. Yes, it is marvellous if we do feel that we are being lifted up into the heavens as we pray; the Bible is not against that. But when that doesn't happen, let us not imagine for one moment that God is not listening. Otherwise, the devil will send us into valleys of discouragement, and we could end up not praying at all! Rather, let us keep praying, even when we don't have wonderful emotional feelings. God is still hearing us. His love and his faithfulness have not abandoned us.

The folly of religious activity

My final warning from this passage concerns the folly of frenzied religious activity apart from God. These Baal prophets expended vast amounts of energy chanting and dancing around the altar for six hours, but to what purpose? They had all this activity, but no fire from heaven. Why? Because it was activity that did not have the blessing and the authority of heaven upon it. As we shall discover, Elijah, on the other hand, called down fire from heaven so that everyone might know that 'I have done all these things at your word' (v. 36). Let the fire fall upon God-directed activity; in truth, it falls nowhere else. One of the saddest things in the church today is feverish activity which has no fire from God because God never ordered it.

We live in days of frenzied religious activity. Christians are running here and there, expending vast amounts of energy, organizing all manner of things—but if the activity is not God-directed and Holy Spirit-led, it is all to no purpose. Some years ago, Dr J. I. Packer wrote these words:

> Modern Christians tend to make busyness their religion. We admire and imitate, and so become, Christian workaholics, supposing that the busiest believers are always the best. Those who love the Lord will indeed be busy for him, no doubt about that; but the spirit of our busyness is constantly wrong. We run around doing things for God and leave ourselves no time for prayer. Yet that does not bother us, for we have forgotten the old adage that if you are too busy to pray you really are too busy. But we do not feel the need to pray, because we have grown

self-confident and self-reliant in our work. We take for granted that our skills and resources and the fine quality of our programmes will of themselves bring forth fruit: we have forgotten that apart from Christ—Christ trusted, obeyed, looked to, relied on—we can achieve nothing (see John 15:5). This is activism: activity gone to seed through not being grounded on sustained self-distrust and dependence on God.[1]

Let us beware the folly of religious activity that is done in the energy of the flesh, not in the power of the Spirit and according to the precepts and the principles of the Word of God.

Note

1 **J.I. Packer,** *Keep in Step with the Spirit* (Leicester: IVP, 1984), p. 98.

Fire from heaven

(1 Kings 18:30–39)

No need to hide

It is now the turn of the prophet Elijah to call upon the name of the Lord God of Israel, so he says to all the people, 'Come near to me' (v. 30). Unlike the false prophets, the true prophet of God is not afraid of close scrutiny. He has nothing to hide. The people can come as close as they like, so that they can see for themselves that there is no trickery. Truth is not afraid of the closest investigation. The devil and his followers love darkness and secrecy, but the genuine Christian should be open and above board. There is no need for cloak-and-dagger activity in the Christian church. We don't have to resort to underhand methods. As the apostle Paul says in 2 Corinthians 4:2, '... we have renounced disgraceful, underhanded ways. We refuse to practise cunning or to tamper with God's word, but by the open statement of the truth we would commend ourselves to everyone's conscience in the sight of God.'

Repairing the altar

We then have a detailed account of Elijah's preparation of the altar and the sacrifice. This is important because in 1 Kings 19:10 we read that the people of Israel had thrown down God's altars—an outward symbol of their idolatry. They had forsaken the true God and turned instead to the worship of Baal. So, when Elijah sets about repairing the altar, he is visibly demonstrating to the people that, before they can expect any blessing from heaven, there must be a renewal of that covenant relationship with the God of Israel, of which the altar was the outward symbol.

The same principle holds good today in the life of every Christian and every church. If we want to see the blessing of Almighty God upon our lives, our homes and our churches, we must make sure that we are in a right relationship with God. Under the New Covenant, this means returning to the foot of the cross and asking the Lord Jesus Christ to cleanse us from sin and disobedience. If you are far away from God because of unconfessed sin, you will never receive any blessing from heaven until you come to Christ and ask for his cleansing and forgiveness on the basis of the cross. The altar must be repaired before God will respond with holy fire.

No need to panic

As we read in verses 31–35 of the elaborate preparations Elijah made, we get the impression of a man who was working very deliberately and methodically. What a contrast to the frenzied wailing and dancing of the Baal prophets! There was no undue haste on the part of Elijah; everything was done decently and in order. If we look back at Leviticus 1:6–8, we find that the prophet was carefully following instructions which the Lord had laid down for the preparation of an acceptable sacrifice. Here the prophet was doing God's work in God's way, so there was no need for any panic or frenzy. The man or woman who is walking in God's will can afford to be calm and patient, because he or she knows that God will honour him or her.

As we saw at the end of the previous chapter, much of the time Christians rush around, getting nowhere fast and wondering why there don't seem to be enough hours in the day. If, however, we follow the example of Elijah and do God's work in God's way, there will always be plenty of time. The trouble is that, all too often, we are not walking closely with the Lord, so we tend to run around in circles.

Longing for God's name to be vindicated

One question that we might ask about these preparations is this: Why the need for water in verses 33–35? On the surface, this seems a bit crazy. Had Elijah taken leave of his senses? The drier the wood, the more likely it was that the fire would take hold of the sacrifice. But this was surely the whole point. Elijah wanted to eliminate all possible suspicion of trickery. He wanted to make it impossible for any fire to consume that sacrifice *apart from* a supernatural intervention by God himself, with the result that the people would be forced to acknowledge the hand of God at work.

We now come to the centrepiece of the passage, the marvellous prayer of Elijah in verses 36 and 37. He begins with the words 'O LORD, God of Abraham, Isaac, and Israel [otherwise known as Jacob]'. This recalls the fact that the Lord had entered into a solemn covenant with Abraham, Isaac and Jacob, and that covenant was a promise that he would be a God to them, and to their descendants after them. This was the foundation of the prayer. As Elijah stands on Mount Carmel, one man against 850 false prophets, he is fully confident because he comes to a God who has promised to keep his covenant with his people. And as we come before the Lord today, facing the opposition of the world, the flesh and the devil, we also need to remind ourselves that we have in heaven a faithful, covenant-keeping God who has said in his Word, 'I will never leave you, nor forsake you' (Hebrews 13:5). This was the source of Elijah's confidence, and it can be ours as well.

The prayer then continues, '... let it be known this day that you are

God in Israel.' The prophet's heart was filled with a burning passion for the glory of God. He did not care about himself, but cared rather about the terrible fact that the people of Israel had renounced Yahweh in favour of Baal. As he says in 19:10, he was 'jealous' for the name of God. His spirit was stirred to the very depths as he considered how the Lord was being so blatantly dishonoured in Israel. So the great burden of his prayer was that the name of God would be vindicated among his people.

One of the marks of our growth in grace is when the glory of God, and the appreciation of that glory by others, becomes a consuming passion in our lives. So often our prayers are selfish. We are so concerned about the success of our work, or the health of our church and families, that we lose sight of the infinitely more important factor, namely, the vindication of Almighty God. This was the supreme concern of the Lord Jesus Christ. For example, in longing for his disciples to bear fruit in their lives, his great desire was that his Father be glorified (John 15:8). What is our motive in wanting people to become Christians and join our churches? Is it so that we can pride ourselves on having large congregations? Perhaps we do have a real concern for people, and we want them to share in the blessings of Christian salvation. This is not a bad motive, but it wasn't the supreme motive of Jesus, or, indeed, of Elijah in this passage. Their greatest desire was for the name of God to be vindicated in the sight of men and women.

If we are honest, we are man-centred in our thinking and our attitudes. It doesn't grieve us that men and women are dishonouring God because of their indifference to his laws. We are more concerned about what they are doing to themselves and to other people as a result of their sin. Elijah, on the other hand, was thoroughly God-centred:

'... let it be known this day that you are God in Israel'; he then continued, '... and that I am your servant, and that I have done all these things at your word'. Elijah wanted the people to know that he wasn't doing all this for the sake of his own ego and reputation; he was a servant of the living God. His own interests were subservient to those of his Master in heaven. Is it our passionate desire to do the will of God, or are we more concerned with doing our own thing? Are our wills so surrendered to our heavenly Father that we can truly say, 'I am your servant'?

Praying with confidence

Because Elijah had acted faithfully in response to his Master's commands, he was confident that the Lord would answer his prayer. This is a very important principle. Jesus said, 'If you abide in me, and my words abide in you, ask whatever you wish, and it will be done for you' (John 15:7). If we are living in a close relationship with God—doing his will and obeying his commandments—we can have the assurance that the Lord will grant our requests. This is because our prayers will inevitably be God-centred, desiring what he wants rather than what we want.

The prophet continues to pray in the same vein in verse 37: 'Answer me, O LORD, answer me, that this people may know that you, O LORD, are God, and that you have turned their hearts back.' Elijah prays that the people will understand that God is a God of sovereign grace. It is not a matter of them making a decision—'It would be nice, wouldn't it, if we worshipped Yahweh.' No. He prays, 'Do this in such a way, Lord, that they will recognize that you have taken the initiative to turn their hearts back from Baal worship.' What a marvellous God-centred prayer! How unlike the way we so often pray! How unlike the ceaseless repetitions of the Baal worshippers! Elijah's prayer is fully rational, intelligent, simple and brief, occupying only two verses in our English Bibles! This reminds us of what we saw in the previous chapter: the acceptability of our prayers does not depend upon the number of words that we use.

God's response

The moment of truth had at last arrived. What a breathless silence there must have been on Mount Carmel! Every eye was fixed on that soaked sacrifice. Then we read in verse 38 that suddenly 'the fire of the LORD fell and consumed the burnt offering'. Notice that the fire didn't leap up from the wood to the sacrifice, which is the normal pattern. This was no ordinary fire; this was supernatural fire from heaven, working its way downwards, contrary to nature. It even consumed the stones and licked up the water in the trench. Whoever heard of ordinary fire doing that?

What was the reaction of the people? Verse 39 says that, 'when all the people saw it, they fell on their faces and said, "The LORD, he is God; the LORD, he is God."'

Does this mean that every single Israelite on Mount Carmel was thoroughly converted to the true God? Sadly not. Subsequent events demonstrate that the people soon forgot what they had seen, and it wasn't long before they relapsed into idolatry. This confession of faith was only superficial. They were forced to make it in the light of the overwhelming evidence before their eyes. They could do nothing else; but it was not a confession of heart-felt repentance and faith. This only serves to underscore a principle mentioned in a previous chapter: miracles, in themselves, have no power to change the hearts of men and women.

The awesome judgement of God

(1 Kings 18:40)

Understanding Elijah's reaction

At the end of the last chapter we found the people of Israel prostrated on the ground, saying, 'The LORD, he is God; the LORD, he is God' (v. 39). However, in the very next verse, we find the prophet Elijah saying something which sounds distinctly jarring to our twenty-first-century ears: 'Seize the prophets of Baal; let not one of them escape.' Then we read that 'they seized them. And Elijah brought them down to the brook Kishon and slaughtered them there.'

This comes as a bit of a shock after what has gone before. We move abruptly from worship in verse 39 to bloody execution in verse 40. In view of the fact that this verse, along with similar verses in the Old Testament, has caused theological problems to some Christians, I will spend a whole chapter attempting to address this issue of judgement. Was Elijah right to slaughter the false prophets? It has been suggested that he was overwrought after the events on Mount Carmel and so, in a fit of pique, he decided to get his own back on his opponents. Is this verse included simply to show us that even the best people make mistakes? Had Elijah gone over the top?

I must state categorically that what the prophet did in verse 40 was carried out with clear scriptural warrant. This is a further example of what he had said in verse 36: 'I have done all these things at your

[God's] word.' The opening verses of Deuteronomy 13 say, 'If a prophet ... arises among you ... and if he says, "Let us go after other gods", which you have not known, and "let us serve them" ... that prophet ... shall be put to death, because he has taught rebellion against the LORD your God ... So you shall purge the evil from your midst.' According to the Old Testament law, if any prophet rose up and turned the people away from the true God, even if he performed miracles, that prophet was to be put to death. So Elijah was acting here in accordance with the clear command of Holy Scripture. He didn't do this because he had a fiery temperament. In fact, the prophet was a very sensitive person, as we saw in Chapter 4. Anyone who treats children and a broken-hearted widow with such tenderness is not a harsh man. But however distasteful this act of execution may have been to Elijah's flesh, he was a servant of the living God. If this is what God had commanded in his Word, so be it. Elijah's emotions were subject to the revealed will of God in Holy Scripture.

Understanding God's command

We might then ask: Why had God given such a command to his people? We can, perhaps, understand the death penalty for murder—but capital punishment for being a false prophet: isn't that taking things too far? Once again, the problem is that we are far too man-centred in our thinking. We consider it somehow acceptable for people to be punished for social offences but not for crimes that affect the honour and the glory of Almighty God. I contend that the Bible has the right perspective here. After all, to be guilty of turning people's hearts away from God is a sin that has eternal consequences. False prophets lead men and women to everlasting ruin in hell. That is a far more serious offence than committing rape or robbing a bank.

However, don't misunderstand me: I'm not suggesting that today we should go around executing false prophets. This was a specific command given to the people of Israel living under the Old Covenant. Only the moral laws of the Old Testament are binding on the Christian conscience, not the civil and criminal laws. However, I do strongly believe that our attitude towards such evil needs to be brought more into line with the Bible's attitude. We should regard the sin of turning people away from God as one of the greatest crimes in the world. Jesus certainly did. He said, '... whoever causes one of these little ones who believe in me to sin, it would be better for him to have a great millstone fastened around his neck and to be drowned in the depth of the sea' (Matthew 18:6).

Let me draw out some principles of application as we seek to relate this to our situation today.

God's sovereignty in judgement

In the first place, we see illustrated here the sovereignty of God in bringing judgement when and how he chooses. The God who has given us life has a right to execute vengeance upon those who have forfeited all claims to life because of their sin. God says, 'Vengeance is mine, I will repay' (Romans 12:19), and you and I have no business quibbling and saying, 'Lord, this isn't fair.' God is sovereign. His ways are not our ways (Isaiah 55:9). Indeed, is it not a wonder that in his patience he withholds his judgement for as long as he does? Far from being astonished that God should pour out his wrath upon these false prophets, we should simply wonder that God had let them loose all those years to pollute the land of Israel! We should marvel at God's patience in temporarily allowing them to turn away the heart of a nation from true worship. After all, if I knew that someone coming to my front door was going to enter my house, rape my wife, kill my children and steal my possessions, I would be very tempted to take precipitate action. Yet Almighty God stood at the door of Israel and, in this human analogy, limited as it is, allowed these false prophets to come in and ravish his special covenant people whom he had redeemed in grace and power. Yes indeed, God was patient and long-suffering.

God's judgement upon false teachers

Secondly, we see illustrated here the righteous judgement of God upon false teachers. Today we live in an age of religious toleration. People tell us that there is no such thing as absolute truth. One person's opinion is as good as another's. We are told that all religions are basically going in the same direction, and that we are all worshipping the same God. That is the spirit of our postmodern age.

However, when we come to the pages of the Bible, the climate is very different. The Bible states clearly that there is an absolute division between truth and error, light and darkness, true prophets and false prophets. Elijah knew that there was such a thing as objective, revealed truth because God had made himself known to his people, and anything else claiming to be truth was a lie. Moreover, anyone who believed such falsehood would be condemned for all eternity. That is the spirit of the Bible; and because Elijah breathed that spirit, he looked upon these false prophets just as God looked upon them. Because the apostle Paul also breathed that spirit, he could say, without any personal pride or vindictiveness, 'But even if we or an angel from heaven should preach to you a gospel contrary to the one we preached to you, let him be accursed' (Galatians 1:8). Paul knew that it doesn't matter how sincere a person is: the real issue is whether he or she is speaking the truth. Sincerity is no test of the genuineness of the product. Either it lines up with what God has revealed in his Word, or it doesn't; and if it doesn't, it is error, which means that it comes under the condemnation and judgement of Almighty God.

Sadly, there are many false teachers in the world today, not only outside the churches, but also within them. If, as I stated earlier, we have no scriptural warrant to execute them, what are we supposed to do about them? Let me mention three things that we can and should be doing as New Testament Christians.

Expose them

Firstly, we are called to expose heresy wherever it raises its ugly head. In Titus 1:9, one of the requirements for being an elder in the church of God is that he be so grounded in sound doctrine that he is able to 'rebuke those who contradict it'. In Revelation 2:2, the Lord Jesus commends the church at Ephesus because they 'have tested those who call themselves apostles and are not, and found them to be false'. Later, in verses 14 and 15 of the same chapter, he rebukes the church at Pergamum for tolerating false teachers in their midst. If there is one thing that causes our Lord holy grief as he looks down upon his church today, it is the flabby toleration of heresy in the ranks of professing Christians. We desperately need to return to New Testament standards of church discipline, in which heresy is ruthlessly exposed.

Do not recognize them as Christians

Secondly, we must give no recognition to heretics as brothers or sisters in Christ. We read these words in 2 John 10–11: 'If anyone comes to you and does not bring this teaching, do not receive him into your house or give him any greeting, for whoever greets him takes part in his wicked works.' In those days, to receive a preacher into your house was to express appreciation of his message, and the exercise of hospitality gave him the material support he needed to spread his views. This doesn't mean that we shouldn't extend common courtesy to a heretic, but it does mean that we should not welcome any such people as fellow-Christians, and we should certainly do nothing whatsoever to encourage or support their ministry.

Proclaim the truth

Thirdly, and more positively, we should seek to destroy error by the proclamation of the truth. We are not called to take up a physical sword to destroy a false prophet, but we can and should take up the sword of the Spirit, 'which is the word of God' (Ephesians 6:17). We should be wholly committed to spreading the truth of God throughout the world by every available means, so that false teaching is cut off and the strongholds of Satan cast down. To that end, we should be praying that God would raise up in our generation men like Elijah who are prepared to preach the pure Word of God with uncompromising boldness. Only as the Word of God is proclaimed in the power of the Holy Spirit will we see the errors of the devil overthrown and the mighty truths of the gospel gloriously upheld.

Further lessons about prayer

(1 Kings 18:41–46)

The people have acknowledged the Lord as the true God of Israel. Elijah, as God's representative, has executed judgement upon the false prophets. Outwardly, the sin of Baal worship has been put away, so now the time has come for the Lord to respond with the blessing of rain. This is always the biblical pattern: sin, the judgement of God, the turning-away from sin, leading to renewed blessing from heaven. We therefore read in verse 41 that 'Elijah said to Ahab, "Go up, eat and drink, for there is a sound of the rushing of rain."' Elijah seems to be saying to Ahab, 'Get on with your carousing because you're not concerned about spiritual matters; but be quick about it, because you might get drenched on the way!'

When the text says 'there is a sound of the rushing of rain', it probably does not mean that Elijah could literally hear the sound of rain. After all, at the time he said it, there was a cloudless blue sky. This is more likely to be an example of what Paul calls 'hearing with faith' (Galatians 3:2). God had promised that rain would come. The prophet therefore believed that rain was on the way, even though he couldn't see any evidence yet with his physical eyes. He was walking by faith, not by sight.

Prayer and God's sovereignty

We read in verse 42 that Ahab went off to indulge his fleshly appetites, while Elijah went up the mountain to pray. Admittedly, this text doesn't actually say that he prayed, although his posture of lowering himself down on the earth and putting his face between his knees gives a pretty fair indication of what he was doing! However, James 5:17–18 makes it crystal clear that Elijah was praying: 'Elijah was a man with a nature like ours, and he prayed fervently that it might not rain, and for three years and six months it did not rain on the earth. Then he prayed again, and heaven gave rain, and the earth bore its fruit.'

Someone might ask, 'If God had promised to send rain, why did the prophet need to pray for it? Surely this prayer was a waste of time, if God was going to send rain anyway.' At this point, we enter one of the deep mysteries of Holy Scripture, namely, the relationship of prayer to the doctrine of God's sovereignty. Although it is true to say that God in his wisdom has decreed that certain events shall come to pass, he has also decreed that these events shall come to pass through appointed means, one of which is prayer. So, instead of prayers being in vain, they are among the means through which God accomplishes his purposes. We might not understand how all that fits together, but no matter; it is our business to get on and pray. Elijah didn't spend his time trying to work out the philosophy behind prayer; he was too busy praying!

How Elijah prayed

We read in verse 42 that he went to the top of Mount Carmel. He deliberately chose to get away from the hubbub and the hurly-burly of the crowds so that he could be alone with his God. He wanted to go somewhere where he was not going to be disturbed, so that he could give himself, body and soul, to the vital task of praying for rain.

This teaches us something very important about prayer. Jesus said in Matthew 6:6, 'But when you pray, go into your room and shut the door and pray to your Father who is in secret. And your father who sees in secret will reward you.' True Spirit-inspired prayer is hard work that demands all our energy, and therefore we have to make sure that other things do not come in to distract us. This is not, of course, to negate the kind of praying that we do when our hands are in the washing-up bowl or as we walk to the train station. That is another kind of praying—sometimes called 'arrow prayers'. But here Elijah is engaged in intercessory prayer for specific needs, and, according to Jesus, that requires the closed door and the secret place.

Notice Elijah's posture. He 'bowed himself down on the earth and put his face between his knees'. The Scriptures record mighty men of God who prayed using different postures. Our Lord himself prayed with his eyes 'lifted up … to heaven' (John 17:1). Paul says that men should pray, 'lifting holy hands' (1 Timothy 2:8). Daniel knelt three times a day to pray (Daniel 6:10). In each case, the posture signifies the attitude of the heart. So it is worth asking: What attitude was signified by this particular posture of Elijah's? Surely it was an attitude of deep reverence and humility in the presence of God.

'But,' someone might say, 'are we not sons and daughters of God? Why do we have to approach God in this cringing way?' This is an important issue which is being debated in the evangelical world at the present time. Although as Christians we are indeed sons and daughters of God, we must never forget that we are still sinners and we are still subjects. Sinners cleansed in the blood of Christ, yes—but sinners still; and the only proper attitude of a sinner in the presence of a holy God is one of humility and brokenness. And though we are sons and daughters, we are still subjects. The Lord is the King, the sovereign on the throne, and the only fitting attitude for a subject in the presence of his or her sovereign is reverence. What a contrast to much of what goes on in the church today! Many of us stroll into the presence of God, with our hands in our pockets. We have so lost sight of the majesty and the holiness of God that we have tended to become over-familiar with him. It is a serious business to have dealings with the almighty Creator God, and there is no room for any shallow frivolity or flippancy.

Let us now consider the actual ingredients contained in this prayer of Elijah's.

A request for a specific blessing

Firstly, there was a specific blessing which Elijah desired from God. It was rain that the parched, cracked land so desperately needed, and it was rain that Elijah looked for when he sent his servant out in verse 43. There was no doubt whatsoever what specific blessing he wanted. How much of our praying is definite and specific? If we are honest, we have to admit that our prayers are often vague and general—'Lord, bless so and so'—without ever zeroing in on the target. We need to be definite, like Elijah. 'Lord, this is the blessing I need; this is the blessing I'll pray for; and I'll look for it until I see it come.'

A pleading of a promise

Secondly, a specific promise was pleaded. Why was Elijah so confident that God was going to answer his prayer? The answer is found in the very first verse of this chapter, where God said to Elijah, 'I will send rain upon the earth.' Elijah was able to plead a specific promise from God; and because of that, he knew that he was praying in accordance with the will of God. This brings us to a very important principle that we should always bear in mind when we pray. Do we have any scriptural warrant to pray for the thing that we are requesting? Or is it the case that, when we get a whim for something, we shoot up a prayer to God and hope for the best? We need to search the Scriptures and ask ourselves whether God has promised to give us the thing for which we are asking. Moreover, if we do have a specific promise, we can then keep praying until we get an answer, because God definitely will answer in his own good time. This is why Elijah was so confident in his praying here.

Persistence and expectancy

Thirdly, Elijah was persistent and expectant before God. We read in verse 43 that he sent his servant to go up and look out over the sea. The servant 'went up and looked and said, "There is nothing."' There was not a cloud in sight! So Elijah sent him again. This happened no fewer than seven times altogether. Now, if we had been in Elijah's shoes, would we not have been tempted to give up after the third or fourth occasion? When we have been specific in our praying, when we have pleaded the promises of God in our praying, when we have looked for an answer and yet have drawn a complete blank, we often give up. We say to ourselves, 'Maybe it's not the Lord's will after all.' Not so Elijah. Because he had a specific promise from God to send rain upon the earth, he persisted in his praying.

Coupled with that persistence was expectation. He sent his servant out seven times to look towards the sea. If God has clearly promised to us certain blessings in his Word, we should go on praying for them until we receive them. Don't give up when the answer doesn't come straight away. Keep on praying, because the Bible teaches that God rewards persistent and expectant prayer.

One question that might be asked is this: If God is going to give us the blessing anyway, why does he make us wait for it? Why didn't God send rain when Elijah first began to pray? Why did God make him wait and send out his servant seven times before he gave the blessing? One of the reasons is that, during such a period of waiting, God wants to do something in the one who is praying. In this episode, God was concerned not only about sending rain, but also about the spiritual life of the prophet Elijah, and he knew that, through this delay, Elijah would learn important lessons about faith, patience and persistence which he would not learn if the answer came immediately.

Are we prepared to wait for God's blessing because we know that, through the delay, God plans to teach us lessons about himself which we would not otherwise learn? God wants to do something in us, in the realm of our sanctification and growth in holy living, which is every bit as important as the immediate blessing for which we are praying. This is why God often delays his answer.

Eventually, the glorious answer did come in response to Elijah's prayers. We read in verse 44 that, at the seventh time of asking, the servant saw 'a little cloud like a man's hand ... rising from the sea'. Before very long, 'the heavens grew black with clouds and wind, and there was a great rain'. We then read that Elijah ran all the way to Jezreel (a distance of some eighteen miles) in front of Ahab's chariot (v. 46). No wonder he was worn out—but more about that in the next chapter!

The cause of depression

(1 Kings 19:1–4)

In 1 Kings 19:1 we read that 'Ahab told Jezebel all that Elijah had done, and how he had killed all the prophets with the sword'. On hearing this, Jezebel sent a message to Elijah, threatening to kill him (v. 2). As a consequence, the prophet was afraid and so ran away to a place called Beersheba, which was apparently about ninety miles away from Mount Carmel (v. 3). He clearly wanted to get as far away from Jezebel as possible. When he arrived at Beersheba, he left his servant there and disappeared into the wilderness, ending up sitting under a broom tree uttering the despondent words, 'It is enough; now, O LORD, take away my life, for I am no better than my fathers' (v. 4).

What were the reasons for the prophet's retreat and his depressive state of mind? I want to suggest four factors.

Physical and emotional exhaustion

Firstly, there was the physical and emotional drain of the past days of ministry. Elijah was completely exhausted. He had spent himself utterly. Consider the emotional stress and strain of his encounter with the prophets of Baal, the intensity of his praying, not to mention that eighteen-mile run to Jezreel in the midst of a blinding rainstorm. The prophet was absolutely drained, emotionally and physically. Often, the reason that we feel depressed is due to a physical cause. Perhaps we have been working too hard. Maybe we are suffering from a heavy cold. It could even simply be that we haven't been getting our regular seven, eight or nine hours of sleep. It is no use telling someone who is physically run-down that the answer to his or her problem is to spend more time in prayer and Bible study! Physical problems need physical remedies. Of course, it is perfectly true that sometimes our physical well-being will affect the state of our souls. For example, if I wake up one morning with a touch of influenza, the devil may use that to attack my faith. However, this does not mean that my problem is basically a spiritual one. Not at all. What I need first and foremost is to spend the day in bed in order to recover my physical strength. I have known times in my Christian life when I have found it very difficult to concentrate when I have been trying to pray and to read the Bible, but a couple of days of going to bed early has changed the whole picture. Let us not run away with the idea that every problem must have a spiritual cause; it just is not so. One of the factors which led to Elijah's depression was the tremendous drain upon his physical frame.

Loneliness

A second factor was plain and simple loneliness. When the Lord questions the prophet in verse 9 of this chapter, Elijah replies, '... I, even I only, am left' (v. 10). He had the sense of being all alone in the great spiritual conflict. Despite the people's outward profession of faith in chapter 18, their response had only been superficial, and now it seemed to Elijah that he was the only faithful Israelite left.

What an illustration this is of the principle expressed in Ecclesiastes 4:9–10: 'Two are better than one ... if they fall, one will lift up his fellow. But woe to him who is alone when he falls and has not another to lift him up!' Human beings need one another. We were not made to live as isolated individuals. This is why God said in Genesis 2:18, 'It is not good that the man should be alone.' Yet here was Elijah, all on his own in his hour of desperate need.

What about that servant of his? Was he not of a sympa and mind towards the prophet? It is hard to know for sur that Elijah left him behind at Beersheba while he took hims the wilderness suggests that something was lacking in their friendship. According to the Bible, 'a brother is born for adversity' (Proverbs 17:17). A true friend is someone, not *from whom* you run, but *to whom* you run in your hour of deepest need. Apparently, therefore, Elijah was without a true friend at this point. How often some of our periods of depression could have been avoided if we had established a deep friendship with another human being! If we are married, then ideally this friendship should be with our spouse. Sadly, however, the ideal is not always realized. It is tragic that many husbands and wives live together under the same roof, yet communicate with each other only at the surface level. Of course, such deep-level communication doesn't just happen; it needs working at. If you are tempted to take the attitude, 'Why bother? I'm happy with the way things are in my marriage', beware. One day, your relationship with your marriage partner could save you from the kind of experience Elijah had when he sat down under the broom tree. Those who are not married need to pray that God will give them someone with whom they can have this kind of friendship and communication.

Blurred spiritual vision

The third reason for Elijah's depression had to do with the blurring of his spiritual vision. In spite of his recent triumph over the enemies of the Lord, he was now terrified by the threats of the queen, so he ran for his life. A man who didn't twitch before a king and a nation now withered in the face of this wicked woman. Why was this? Surely it was partly because he was suffering from a blurring of his spiritual perspective. When he was up on the mountain, he had his eyes firmly fixed on the living God who supported and sustained him; as long as he had that perspective, he was invincible. However, once that vision was blurred, he showed that he had feet of clay.

This reminds us of the apostle Peter walking on the water. As long as he was looking at Jesus, he stayed afloat in the midst of the raging sea. But once he took his eyes off the Lord and focused instead on the wind and the waves, he started to sink (Matthew 14:30).

What a vital lesson this is! As Christians, we need to look beyond the immediate problems that threaten to overwhelm us. To concentrate on the problems is what the Bible calls walking by sight and not by faith (see 2 Corinthians 5:7). This is fatal, both to our peace of mind and to our spiritual well-being. However desperate and unpleasant our circumstances, we need to realize that God is in control. He is with us to support us, and he will not let us down. We need to echo that plea of the first disciples of Jesus: 'Increase our faith!' (Luke 17:5). Faith is the great antidote to fear. If we are really trusting in God and believing his promises, then, when problems arise, we shall face them with courage and contentment.

Disappointment and frustration

A fourth reason for Elijah's depression was his disappointed hopes and frustrated expectations. Elijah had just come from a situation in which he had seen the defeat of the prophets of Baal. He had seen the vindication of the true God on Mount Carmel. He had seen a whole nation cry out, 'The LORD, he is God; the LORD, he is God' (18:39). He had seen the heavens open and the rains come thundering down. If we had seen all that, would we not be tempted to think that some great spiritual blessing was just around the corner? 'Surely this is the beginning of a great movement of God that is going to sweep through the entire nation,' we might think. Yet, in the midst of all these hopes and expectations, a servant arrives from the king's palace, saying, 'This time tomorrow, Elijah, your blood will be mixed with that of those Baal prophets!' All the prophet's hopes and expectations come crashing to the ground. Proverbs 13:12 says, 'Hope deferred makes the heart sick.' This was surely Elijah's experience here.

What Elijah failed to realize was that the work begun on Mount Carmel would take time. He thought that revival was going to begin immediately. However, God had other plans that extended beyond Elijah. This is brought out in 19:15–18, where God commands Elijah to go and anoint Jehu as king of Israel, the one who would carry out the work of reform and kill the last of the Baal worshippers. God had long-term plans which Elijah didn't appreciate or understand. (We will look at this in detail in Chapter 13.) In the meantime, Elijah should have realized that God was still on the throne. Instead, he was so taken up with the affairs of the present that he thought that everything he had done was a complete waste of time.

If we are to be kept from these Elijah-like experiences of depression, we too need to remember that our God has long-term plans and purposes which are outside the circle of what we can immediately see. Elijah looked around and said to himself, 'Nothing's happening any more. Everything's come to a grinding halt. What's the point of going on?' But this was a grave misjudgement of the situation. We must never measure what we think God is doing by that which we have actually seen him do. The measure of God's work is not what *we* see, but what *God* sees. Some of God's most beautiful plants and flowers are to be found out in the middle of deserts, where nobody sees them except God himself, and what is true in the realm of nature is also true in the realm of grace. God has plans for his church about which we know absolutely nothing. Perhaps when we get to heaven we will meet up with long-lost relatives whom we discover were genuine born-again Christians, and we never knew about it. The important thing is that God knows! If we measure the extent of God's working by what we actually see and know, we shall reach rock-bottom in discouragement.

Instead, let us affirm with the prophet Habakkuk,

> Though the fig tree should not blossom,
>   nor fruit be on the vines,
> the produce of the olive fail
>   and the fields yield no food,
> the flock be cut off from the fold
>   and there be no herd in the stalls,
> yet I will rejoice in the LORD;
>   I will take joy in the God of my salvation.
> GOD, the Lord, is my strength …
> (Habakkuk 3:17–19a)

In spite of all the problems and difficulties that we see around us, we need to remember that the Lord has promised to be with his people and never to forsake them. He has said that no labour in his name will ever be in vain (1 Corinthians 15:58), and 'in due season we will reap, if we do not give up' (Galatians 6:9).

Remedies for depression

(1 Kings 19:5–8)

When Elijah said in 19:4 'LORD, take away my life', the Lord didn't answer this prayer because it was one that was full of sin and self-pity. Thank God that he doesn't answer all our prayers. As we think back over some of the prayers we have uttered over the years, are we not profoundly grateful that God hasn't answered all of them? If he had done so, we would have been in a lot of trouble, because what we want is not always what is right for us. This was certainly the case for Elijah here. Instead of giving Elijah what he prayed for, what did the Lord do?

He assured him of his love

Firstly, he assured the prophet of his tender love and concern. We read in verse 5 that he sent an angel to touch him. This is quite remarkable. Here is Elijah, out in the wilderness, a day's journey from his servant and almost 100 miles from his last place of triumph, totally dejected and depressed—and he wakes up to find an angel standing in front of him! It is as if God was saying to the prophet, 'Elijah, even though you're out here in the middle of nowhere, I want to assure you that you have not wandered beyond the sight of my eye, nor beyond the love of my heart.' The very presence of the angel was an assurance of God's tender love and concern.

Notice the way the angel treated Elijah. We are told in verse 5 that the angel 'touched him'. In verse 7, we read, 'the angel of the LORD came a second time and touched him.' A similar incident happens in the New Testament, in Acts 12. Peter is sleeping in prison, and an angel strikes him on the side, saying, 'Get up quickly' (v. 7). I suggest that there is a difference between being 'struck' and being 'touched'. One indicates firmness, the other, gentleness. In Peter's case, time was pressing, so the angel needed to give him a good whack to get him moving quickly. In Elijah's case, the touch was one of gentleness in order to indicate God's tender love and concern.

Is this not a wonderful scenario? Here is the prophet in a state of rebellion and disobedience, and the very first thing the Lord does is not rebuke him and tell him that he has no business running away; instead, he assures him of his gracious love and compassion. We shall return to this theme later.

He provided for his physical needs

The second thing the Lord did for Elijah was provide for his immediate physical needs of food and rest. We are told in verse 6 that the prophet 'looked, and behold, there was at his head a cake baked on hot stones and a jar of water. And he ate and drank and lay down again.' God cares about our bodies as well as about our souls. It is very interesting to note that God wanted to give Elijah food and rest before he challenged him about spiritual issues. In due course, the Lord was going to deal with the prophet's sin. He was going to probe his conscience and face him with the fact that he had no business being out there in the wilderness. He was going to ask twice in verses 9 and 13, 'What are you doing here, Elijah?' However, God knows that we are not fit to grapple with deep spiritual issues if we are in a state of physical imbalance. We saw in the previous chapter that the whole world can look a different place after a good night's sleep. God understands that. He has made the human body the way it is, and if we ignore what he has made, we will suffer for it. We cannot, for example, go on overworking indefinitely without suffering the consequences. The time comes when we must either delegate or drop some of our commitments; otherwise, we will crack up and we will be of no use to anybody. A French philosopher once said, 'I have so much to do that I must go to bed!'

Before we go any further, it is worth asking the question: Who was this angel? He is described as 'the angel of the LORD' (v. 7). This is a special title for a special angel. If we look up references to him throughout the Old Testament, we find that this angel, unlike other angels, is virtually identified with God, being an extension of the divine personality, and he speaks not only in the name of God, but as God himself, in the first person singular. In view of this, some Bible scholars argue that this special angel of the Lord was none other than a pre-incarnate manifestation of the Lord Jesus Christ himself. I would not want to be dogmatic about this, but if there is truth in this argument, then we have here a beautiful illustration of the Lord Jesus fulfilling that ministry of which Isaiah spoke concerning the Messiah: 'a bruised reed he will not break, and a faintly burning wick he will not quench' (42:3). In other words, anyone who is near to exhaustion God will treat with tender love and concern. Surely, if ever a man was near to exhaustion, it was the prophet Elijah in this passage; and along came the Lord with all the gentleness of his love and compassion, ministering tenderly to his servant.

How often have we been like Elijah? Instead of the Lord coming down upon us and immediately chastising us for our disobedience, he has assured us of his love and concern, and stooped to minister to our needs.

I strongly believe that in these verses we also have a picture of how the Lord would have us deal with one another in the Christian church. It is true that there is a time when sin needs to be rebuked and we must follow the instructions Paul gives in 2 Thessalonians 3:14: 'If anyone does not obey what we say in this letter, take note of that person, and have nothing to do with him.' However, when someone who has given positive evidence of spiritual life is sitting under a broom tree of dejection and depression, what is the very first thing that the Lord does? He does not rap that person over the knuckles and probe his or her conscience. On the contrary, he comes alongside that person in gentleness and loving concern. What an important lesson for us to learn as Christians! Psychologists tell us that before we rebuke and criticize, we need first to build the bridge of empathy and understanding. This is not at all an unscriptural idea, as we can see from this passage.

We read in Luke 22:61 that, after Peter denied Jesus three times, 'the Lord turned and looked at Peter'. Did he look with a frown of righteous anger? I can't prove it, but I very much suspect that he had a look of gentle love and compassion, which is why Peter went out and wept bitterly. Someone has rightly said, 'The assurance of the love of God, in spite of our sins, is the surest way to break our hearts for our sins.' Think of your own Christian experience. Isn't this what breaks us more than anything else—when God gives us a glance showing his love and compassion?

We need to plead with God that he would give us this attitude towards one another. Galatians 5:22–23 tells us that 'love' and 'gentleness' are part of the fruit of the Holy Spirit. This is not something we can achieve in the energy of the flesh. Left to ourselves, either we sinfully tolerate what should be condemned and rebuked, or, like the Pharisees, we condemn those with whom we should be gentle.

We either excuse sin in our fellow-Christians, or go around finger-wagging in a spirit of hypocritical superiority. It is so difficult to maintain the balance of Scripture. We therefore need to ask God to crucify that which is natural in us, and to give us instead the supernatural grace and fruit of Holy Spirit-inspired love and gentleness. We also need the Spirit's wisdom to know how and when such grace should be exercised.

I would be surprised if these principles haven't reminded us of the Parable of the Prodigal Son in Luke 15. The son went off into the haunts of sin and wickedness, using up his father's hard-earned money in the process. Yet, when the father saw him returning in the distance, he had compassion, and 'he ran and embraced him and kissed him' (15:20). The father made it very obvious that he loved his son. One of the hardest things for us to believe as children of God, when we are sitting under a broom tree, is that God loves us in that condition. It is not hard to believe that God should chastise and rebuke me, but to believe that God still loves me in spite of my sin and disobedience—that is difficult. That is when faith needs to be exercised at its strongest.

It was relatively easy for Elijah to believe that God loved him when he was up on Mount Carmel, vindicating God's name and slaying those Baal prophets. But when he found himself in a state of disobedience and dejection and then saw a messenger of God who, rather than putting out his hand to rebuke him, instead gave him assurance of the grace and the tender mercy of the Lord, that was really hard for Elijah to believe. What an astonishingly compassionate God we have as our loving heavenly Father!

If anyone uses a passage like this as an excuse to sin, he or she has not understood the first thing about Christian salvation. A man or woman who has grasped something of the love of God in Christ and who is indwelt by the Holy Spirit will not want to run wilfully into the paths of sin and disobedience. Moreover, this is only half of God's dealings with Elijah—as we shall discover in the next chapter!

Further remedies for depression

(1 Kings 19:9–18)

God made him examine himself

After the second visit from the angel and the provision of more food, Elijah arose and went in the strength of that food to a place called Horeb, the mountain of God (19:4). Horeb, of course, was the place where God had appeared to Moses in the burning bush. It was also the place where God had given the law to Israel. Why did the prophet choose to go to Horeb? Nobody can say for sure. It seems unlikely that the angel had told him to go there, because the word of the Lord came to him in verse 9, saying, 'What are you doing here, Elijah?' The implication of that question is, 'Elijah, you're not here because I sent you here.' It seems that the prophet decided off his own bat to continue his travels through the wilderness, until eventually he arrived at Horeb, the mountain of God.

We saw in the previous chapter that God's first dealings with Elijah in his state of depression consisted of tender love and concern. God did not challenge his prophet until he had had sufficient food and rest. However, now that Elijah had been physically restored, the time had come for a probing question: 'What are you doing here, Elijah?' This question would have forced the prophet to retrace in his mind all the steps that had brought him to this cave. It would have encouraged him to stop in his tracks and say to himself, 'What on earth am I doing here, and how did I get here?' Elijah had become so immersed in dejection and unbelief that he had become almost like a drunken man, reeling to and fro and moving from place to place without gathering his spiritual wits about him. By asking this question, the Lord wanted the prophet to face up to his true spiritual condition.

Very often, when we are in a state of sin and disobedience, one of the first steps to restored fellowship with God is a serious self-examination of our present state in the light of Scripture. Perhaps you need to do that very thing now. In Psalm 119:59, we read, 'When I think on my ways, I turn my feet to your testimonies.' The first indication of a return to the father by the prodigal son is recorded with the words 'he came to himself' (Luke 15:17). There was self-reflection that finally brought everything into its proper perspective, and the son saw what a fool he had been. As we ponder this, it may be that God will use it to probe our consciences and then lead us back to a place of usefulness, where once again we are walking in the light of his revealed will. This was certainly the case with Elijah, as we shall now see.

God showed him that he was still working

Having challenged him with the uncomfortable question of verse 9, the Lord tells Elijah to stand upon the mountain (v. 11). Then 'a great and strong wind' comes along, followed by an earthquake and a fire. The text tells us that the Lord is in none of these dramatic manifestations (vv. 11–12). However, after the fire comes 'the sound of a low whisper' (v. 12), or, in the words of older translations, 'a still small voice' (KJV).

What was the significance of all this? It is not possible to be absolutely certain, but the lesson could be this: God has ways of working other than the dramatic and the spectacular. Elijah thought that the Lord was going to come along like a mighty wind and immediately sweep away all the idolatry from Israel. But, despite the dramatic happenings on Mount Carmel, Ahab seemed to be just the same, Jezebel was as defiant as ever and the nation had not been brought to true repentance. So Elijah had come to the conclusion that God must have gone to sleep on the job—'The Lord has stopped working.'

It is always fatal to think that God works only through mighty upheavals. Sometimes, he works by means of 'a low whisper'. Just because there aren't dramatic happenings, it doesn't mean that the Lord is not still carrying out his sovereign plans and purposes in the lives of men and women. This was a vital lesson for Elijah to learn, and it is a lesson we need to lay hold of in our own day. By all means, let us pray that God will visit his people in dramatic and exciting ways. Praise God for the day of Pentecost; praise him for the eighteenth-century revival. But, at the same time, when there is no wind and fire, let us not get depressed and discouraged. God is still working out his purposes, albeit silently and imperceptibly. And let us certainly not seek to manufacture our own wind and fire in the energy of the flesh.

God revealed to him his plans

In verses 15–18, God reveals to his prophet that he has long-term plans and purposes for Israel which Elijah has simply not understood. 'Go,' says the Lord, 'return on your way to the wilderness of Damascus. And when you arrive, you shall anoint Hazael to be king over Syria. And Jehu the son of Nimshi you shall anoint to be king over Israel, and Elisha the son of Shaphat of Abel-meholah you shall anoint to be prophet in your place' (vv. 15–16).

HE GAVE HIM A TASK TO DO

The first thing to notice here is that God gives Elijah a specific task to accomplish. The prophet had been spending his time in solitude. Verse 8 tells us that he was wandering in the wilderness forty days and forty nights. Then, as we saw in verse 9, this was followed by a probing of his conscience and a time for reflection and self-examination. So Elijah had been in a state of passivity and inaction for some time. Such periods are sometimes necessary. However, if the prophet was to be restored to spiritual vitality, he needed once again to be found in the place of activity in the kingdom of God. This is why God gave him a specific task to do.

Having a God-given task to do can be a very important means of grace in restoring a discouraged servant of Christ. A stagnant pool becomes polluted, but a running stream cleanses itself of unpleasant weeds and smells; and so it is in the life of the child of God. Those believers who refuse to be involved in active Christian responsibility become more and more polluted with their own spiritual stagnancy, and it is not at all surprising if they become depressed. Very often, one finds with depressed folk that their areas of concern have become narrowed down to themselves, whereas if they were actively involved in the concerns of God's kingdom and of other people, they would not be able to afford the luxury of retreating into depression.

Some believers have many weighty responsibilities, whether at work, at home or in the life of the church. At times, we can become weary and wish that our burden was lighter. But have we ever stopped to thank God for these responsibilities because they could be the very means of preventing us from sitting down under a broom tree of despair and dejection? Those who don't have such responsibilities should, perhaps, be praying that God would show them what task he would have them do in the work of the kingdom—a task with which they can become so involved that they have no time for depression!

HE ENCOURAGED HIM

But not only does God give Elijah a job to do; he also gives him a twofold encouragement as he steps out to perform the task.

The reformation would be completed

On the one hand, God tells Elijah that the work of reformation will be completed in Israel: '… the one who escapes from the sword of Hazael shall Jehu put to death, and the one who escapes from the sword of Jehu shall Elisha put to death.' Hazael was a heathen king whom God would use as an instrument of judgement upon Israel for their idolatry. Jehu was a king of Israel who was filled with a consuming passion to blot out the house of Ahab. As for Elisha, we have no record that he actually took up the sword to slay anybody, so perhaps metaphorical language is being used here. His prophetic ministry was certainly one that would cut and wound, exposing sin and destroying evil. So the Lord was assuring Elijah that, by means of these three men, the work of reformation would be completed, and Baal worship would finally be exterminated from Israel.

This must have been a great encouragement to the prophet, who had thought that all was lost and that God wasn't interested any more. If ever we feel despondent and discouraged, like Elijah, because our best efforts seem to be getting nowhere, let us always remember that God's work will continue, even if we never live to see the fruit of our labours. Elijah would never personally witness the final destruction of Baal worship in Israel. That was a privilege which God had reserved for his successors. The principle that operates in such cases is 'One sows and another reaps' (John 4:37). In this life we are called to be faithful, not successful. Our responsibility is to do what God commands, and to leave the results in his hands. A Christian minister may labour for twenty years in a church and see little visible fruit. That doesn't matter if he has been faithful to the Lord. It may well be that his successor will reap a great harvest from all the seed that has been sown. This was an important part of the message of hope and encouragement which the Lord gave to Elijah.

A remnant would be reserved

The second word of encouragement comes in verse 18: 'I will leave seven thousand in Israel, all the knees that have not bowed to Baal, and every mouth that has not kissed him.' Elijah is assured that even when the work of reformation is done and Baal worship is finally exterminated, there will still be 7,000 people in Israel whom God has reserved as a faithful, believing remnant—'a remnant, chosen by grace', as Paul says in Romans 11:5. God had no intention of abandoning Israel to the devil. He had his people, chosen before the foundation of the world, whom he would preserve, even in the midst of all this dreadful apostasy. As Jesus said, '... I will build my church, and the gates of hell shall not prevail against it' (Matthew 16:18).

This is surely a principle we need to grasp in our own days as we see evil and wickedness abounding on all sides. We need to take encouragement from the fact that God has his elect in every tribe, tongue, people and nation, whom he will definitely save and bring to a knowledge of himself. There is nothing the devil can ever do which will prevent God from fulfilling his sovereign purposes of saving men and women. Speaking personally, this is one of the great truths that keeps me going in the Christian ministry in the midst of all the disappointments and frustrations. God is sovereign, and he has a people whom he *will* bring to Christ, through the operation of the Holy Spirit. 'All that the Father gives me will come to me,' said Jesus (John 6:37). There is no doubt about it.

What a tremendous encouragement this would have been to Elijah! He thought that the work of grace was finished in Israel, but God assured him that this was far from being the case. God's great plan of salvation would continue. The work of the kingdom would ultimately triumph. What a glorious perspective! Does not this great spiritual vision give us a real desire to throw ourselves into God's work, body and soul? After all, if God's plans and purposes cannot fail, and I am identified with such a God, what room is there for depression?

Chapter 14

The slavery of sin

(1 Kings 21)

The fact that Elijah was fully restored to God's service is made clear in 19:19–21, where we read of Elisha's call to the prophetic ministry. Immediately after God's instructions in verses 15–18, Elijah went off to find his successor. There was no trace of any jealousy here. If we had been in Elijah's shoes, perhaps we might have been tempted to resent the fact that someone else was to take our place as a prophet in Israel; but Elijah seemed quite happy to cast his cloak upon Elisha as an outward sign of the succession. We then hear nothing further about Elijah until 21:17 and the well-known story of Naboth's vineyard.

This is a classic tale of greed and corruption. Ahab wants to acquire a vineyard that belongs to a man called Naboth. Naboth refuses because, he says in verse 3, it is 'the inheritance of my fathers'. God had, in fact, expressly forbidden the people of Israel to buy and sell the land which he had given to them (see Leviticus 25:23). So Naboth isn't being deliberately obstreperous here; he is obeying a clear command of the Lord.

Jezebel then enters the scene and schemes to acquire the vineyard by wicked means. She plots to have Naboth stoned to death on a trumped-up charge, which gives Ahab the opportunity to seize the vineyard. However, that is not the end of the story because we read in verses 17–19 that the prophet Elijah is commanded to pronounce a fearful message of judgement upon both Ahab and Jezebel. This is such a serious and sober story of sin and judgement that we will spend two chapters considering the many lessons of warning that we need to heed.

Sin is a cruel taskmaster

Consider how cruel is sin as a taskmaster. When sin is lord and master, it acts like Pharaoh in Egypt, who brought the whip down upon the Israelites in bondage and made their lives thoroughly miserable. This was certainly the case with Ahab, who, when he couldn't get what he wanted, went into his house vexed and sullen. He then lay down on his bed, turned away his face and refused to eat any food (v. 4). This analogy of a cruel taskmaster is precisely the image of sin which we find portrayed in verse 20, where Elijah says to Ahab, '... you have sold yourself to do what is evil in the sight of the LORD'. Here is a man who gave himself body and soul to be a willing slave of the devil, and, when he did so, found that the devil is no Christian and no gentleman! When Ahab sold himself to evil, no doubt he anticipated that he would find pleasure and fulfilment. However, verse 4 gives us the picture of a man who is mentally and emotionally distraught. Sin, although initially attractive, always leads to grief and misery.

Sin turns us into scheming fiends

The genius of the human mind can become the instrument of fiendish activity when it is under the power of sin. Jezebel's plan is a masterpiece of intrigue and deception. When we give ourselves to a lie, it is extraordinary how our God-given mental powers can be used to work out all sorts of schemes for covering our tracks. None of us is immune from this; not even the great King David of Israel, who wrote many of the psalms. Remember how he plotted and schemed to have Bathsheba's husband killed. Each of us can fall, and at any time. Let us not play with e cock-sure with self-confidence. 'Therefore let anyone who t he stands take heed lest he fall' (1 Corinthians 10:12).

Sin turns us into weak-willed jelly-fish

In verse 25, we read that Ahab was a man 'whom Jezebel his wife incited'. Ahab was a wicked man, but his wickedness would not have progressed as far as it did without the incitement of his wife. She stirred him up. Likewise, if we, as Christians, give any ground to sin in our lives, we easily become spineless and gutless. Every time we see evil perpetrated and we keep quiet, sin has made us into unprincipled jelly-fish, more concerned about our own reputations than with the honour and glory of Almighty God. One of the marks of being filled with the Holy Spirit is that we have nerves of steel when it comes to moral principles, and we stand firm against any opposition once the path of duty has been made plain.

Sin deceives us about our relationships

Sin makes us look upon our best friends as our worst enemies, and vice versa. In verse 20, Ahab said to Elijah, 'Have you found me, O my enemy?' Yet, when Jezebel had entered the room in verse 15 and started to flash her eye-lashes, Ahab had given her rapt attention. This wicked woman, Jezebel, was the one who had incited him to evil, the result of which would be the frustration of his ambitions, the extermination of his sons and his own miserable death. However, sin so perverted his judgement and affections that Ahab regarded Jezebel as his best friend. Elijah was really his best friend, because he was God's instrument to call him to repentance; yet Ahab regarded him as his worst enemy. Sin can do just the same for us today.

Those people at work who tell us the latest immoral jokes; those neighbours whose conversation and whose moral principles are anti-Christian—such people are not our best friends. We may think they are, but nothing could be further from the truth. Anyone who by word or example encourages us to go on one moment longer in a state of rebellion and hypocrisy is our worst enemy. To put it bluntly, such folk are co-operating with the devil to poison our souls. Who are truly our best friends? Those Christians who continually encourage us along the hard and narrow path that leads to eternal life. We may be tempted to think that they are narrow-minded bigots who only want to stop us enjoying ourselves, but in reality they are the best friends that we could ever have. But sin so corrupts and twists our hearts that we sometimes find ourselves, like Ahab, welcoming those who want to incite us to evil, and despising those who are trying to steer us into the paths of righteousness.

Think of this principle in the realm of the pulpit. Who is our best friend in the pulpit? Is it the preacher who tells us smooth and pleasant things all the time? Is it the preacher who is always saying that God loves us and that the Lord is kind and patient? Certainly, those truths are in the Bible, but surely our best friend in the pulpit is not the person who makes us feel good week after week; rather, it is the person who tells us the truth of God about ourselves. Our best friend in the pulpit is the one who tells us that unconfessed sin is like a cancer eating away at our souls, and who wants the grace of God to remove that cancer. He does not want to spread the Vaseline of religious platitudes all over it. Yet sin will so pervert us that we regard our best friends as our worst enemies, and our worst enemies as our best friends.

Sin misuses the Word of God

Sin will make us use even the Word of God for wicked ends. Isn't this what Jezebel was doing in verse 10? She had enough acquaintance with the Old Testament Scriptures to know that, if Naboth was to be strung up on a charge of blasphemy, she needed at least two or three witnesses. That was the requirement of the Word of God. So she says, '... set two worthless men opposite him, and let them bring a charge against him, saying, "You have cursed God and the king."'

Did Jezebel really care about blaspheming the name of Almighty God? After all, she was a Baal worshipper. Yet here she used even the Word of God to accomplish her own wicked purposes, and this is what sin will sometimes do in the human heart. For example, the Bible says that God loves us, and that if we put our trust in the Lord Jesus Christ, all our sins are forgiven—past, present and future. But then the devil comes along and whispers in our ears, 'Isn't that wonderful? Because all sin is forgiven, you can sin as much as you like', and so the great truths of the grace of God are twisted into a licence to sin. Paul had to deal with this very problem when, at the beginning of Romans 6, he posed the question, 'Are we to continue in sin that grace may abound?' The answer, of course, is a resounding 'By no means!'

The Bible also says that, as New Covenant Christians, we have been 'released from the law' (Romans 7:6), yet the devil uses that to tell us that we are no longer obliged to keep the moral laws of God. 'You are free to pander to the desires of the flesh,' he says. Of course, what Paul meant by using those words is that, if we belong to Christ, we have been released from the condemnation of the law.

Let us beware if Scriptures are suggested to us when we are contemplating some way to excuse sin or avoid repentance. If the devil could quote verses to Jesus when he was in the wilderness (see Matthew 4:6), he can certainly do the same to us. Sin is such a foul, polluting influence that it will make a person use even the Word of God for evil ends.

What a terrible picture is portrayed in this passage of the dreadful effects of sin upon the human soul! Lest we become unduly discouraged, let me close this chapter with the reminder that deliverance is gloriously possible. The angel said to Joseph in a dream, '... you shall call his name Jesus, for he will save his people from their sins' (Matthew 1:21). The good news of the gospel is that there is someone who can rescue us, not just from the *guilt* of sin, but also from the captivating *power* of sin in our lives. He can check its influence and cleanse it from our hearts. The Lord Jesus Christ is the mighty deliverer. Let us call upon him to help us in this great conflict.

Chapter 15

Day of reckoning

(1 Kings 21)

Unholy marriage alliances

In the previous chapter, we examined the insidious influence of sin upon the lives of Ahab and Jezebel. Before we go on to consider God's attitude to such wickedness, it is worth contemplating Ahab's marriage. If the king could have foreseen all the terrible judgements that were to come, not only upon himself but also upon his entire household, as a direct consequence of his involvement with Jezebel, would he have married this evil woman? Of course not! No man in his right mind would have done so. Why, then, did Ahab marry Jezebel? There are two possible reasons. On the one hand, there was the advancement of his own personal interests and ambitions. He might have reasoned that, if he married the daughter of the king of the Sidonians, it would put him in a good relationship with a neighbouring heathen nation. On the other hand, there was also the undoubted physical attraction of Jezebel. We have a hint of this in 2 Kings 9:30, where we read how she dressed herself up and made eyes at Jehu through the window.

As the devil attempts to destroy the lives of Christian men and women today, one of the most powerful means he uses is unholy marriage alliances, in spite of clear Scriptures like 2 Corinthians 6:14, where Paul says, 'Do not be unequally yoked with unbelievers.' If you are contemplating marriage, and all you are thinking about are your personal lusts and ambitions, beware lest you are being used as a pawn on the devil's chessboard. His goal is never our ultimate happiness, but rather our eternal ruin. What a difference it would have made to Ahab if Jezebel had actually encouraged him in the things of God! If only the king had had a godly wife who could have pushed him in the right direction! Instead, at every turn, she stirred him up to more and more wickedness.

If you are thinking about marriage, don't simply look for a man or woman who is a professing Christian. Ask God to give you someone in whose heart the Lord Jesus Christ reigns as Lord and King. Otherwise, the time will undoubtedly come when there is a conflict of loyalties, and, instead of your partner encouraging you to seek first the kingdom of God, he or she will subtly try to steer you away from God-given priorities.

How did God view the machinations of Ahab and Jezebel in this passage? Elijah tells us in verses 20–24.

God sees everything

The first thing to note is that Ahab had done 'what is evil in the sight of the LORD' (v. 20). The Bible tells us that God sees everything and knows everything. No doubt Ahab knew this in his mind as a theological proposition; but a person can know the truth intellectually and still be relatively at ease in his or her sin. However, if you are standing in the middle of a Naboth's vineyard, thinking that you have committed the perfect crime and that no one knows, and then you turn round and see an Elijah, who points his finger at you and says, 'God knows'—at that point, the breath goes out of you and the blood drains from your face, and you are suddenly gripped with the haunting reality that God knows everything.

Maybe you are reading these words and have congratulated yourself that you have perpetrated the perfect lie, and you have foolishly thought, 'No one knows.' Weeks and months have passed since you told the lie, so it has almost become buried in your memory, but even now it is beginning to resurrect itself. In the sight of God, that lie is as fresh as if it had just fallen from your lips in the last ten seconds. The Lord Jesus Christ spoke clearly on this subject in Luke 12:1–3: 'Beware of the leaven of the Pharisees, which is hypocrisy. Nothing is covered up that will not be revealed, or hidden that will not be known. Therefore whatever you have said in the dark shall be heard in the light, and what you have whispered in private rooms shall be proclaimed on the housetops.'

God will fulfil his promises of judgement

Following this, Elijah declared to Ahab that God would eventually fulfil all his promises of judgement. He prophesied, firstly, that Ahab would be killed and the dogs would lick his blood (v. 19). Secondly, all Ahab's household would be exterminated (vv. 21–22). Thirdly, wicked queen Jezebel would herself be eaten up by dogs (v. 23). If we read through the rest of 1 and 2 Kings, we find that all three predictions were fulfilled, right down to the very last letter. It makes for gory reading, but it does illustrate the inescapable truth that God will eventually fulfil all his promises of judgement upon wicked men and women. As someone has said, 'Though the wheels of God's judgement appear to grind slowly, in the end they grind to powder.' When she was gloating over the death of Naboth, little did Jezebel know that, before too long, dogs would be licking their lips because of her flesh which they had just devoured. The same God who predicted these awful judgements upon Ahab and Jezebel has also clearly said in his Word that the final destiny of every unrepentant sinner is everlasting punishment in hell (2 Thessalonians 1:7–9). What God prophesies always comes to pass.

Ahab's response

When Ahab heard these terrible words of judgement, 'he tore his clothes and put sackcloth on his flesh and fasted and lay in sackcloth and went about dejectedly'. On the surface, this seems to be quite impressive. But we need to ask the question: Was this a true repentance on the part of the king? And how is it possible to tell? Jesus said, '... you will recognize them by their fruits' (Matthew 7:20). In Acts 26:20, Paul said, '... they [Jews and Gentiles] should repent and turn to God, performing deeds in keeping with their repentance.' Judged by this yardstick, do we have reason to believe that Ahab's repentance was true or false? If we read 1 Kings 22, it is apparent that Ahab's response to God's Word was only a surface reaction. In 22:8, Ahab says to a man called Jehoshaphat, 'There is yet one man by whom we may enquire of the LORD, Micaiah the son of Imlah, but I hate him, for he never prophesies good concerning me, but evil.' Jehoshaphat then replies, 'Let not the king say so'; later, in verse 27, Ahab actually orders Micaiah to be imprisoned because he has given the king an unwelcome prophecy.

It is quite clear, therefore, that Ahab's repentance was only a very shallow thing. He was initially disturbed by the judgements to come, as prophesied against himself and his family. But then in 21:29, God said, 'Have you seen how Ahab has humbled himself before me? Because he has humbled himself before me, I will not bring the disaster in his days; but in his son's days I will bring the disaster upon his house.' Although God will eventually judge the wicked, he is also long-suffering and merciful. God never enjoys executing his judgements, when he sees a little surface repentance on the part of Ahab, he says, 'I take note of that, and I'm going to delay the full measure of my judgement for a period.' As a consequence, Ahab did not live to see the destruction of all his sons, which he otherwise would have done.

The important point is this: when God decided to delay his judgements, Ahab started to breathe more easily again, and in chapter 22 he reverted to his former attitude of disrespect and rebellion against the word of God through the prophet Micaiah. Here is surely an acid test of the genuineness of our repentance: Has it changed our basic attitude to the authority of the living God, as expressed in his Word? However much people may tremble at the thoughts of hell to come, and, like Ahab, go through some very impressive outward rituals, when the dust has settled can they say with the psalmist, 'My soul keeps your testimonies; I love them exceedingly. I keep your precepts and testimonies, for all my ways are before you' (Psalm 119:167–168)? Jesus said, 'If you love me, you will keep my commandments' (John 14:15). The mark of a true Christian is subjection to the Word of God, because it is the Word of the God whom we have been brought to love and trust.

There is much superficiality in the Christian church today. We are tempted to look at things only in the short term. We see, for example, a crowded church and we say to ourselves, 'There must be a real work of God going on here!' We think that a lot of people and a lot of activity inevitably spell success. However, that is only a superficial understanding. The real test of a successful church is not to be found in the numbers of people who attend the meetings, but rather in their attitude to the Word of God. Are they—to use words from the Parable of the Sower—'those who, hearing the word, hold it fast in an honest and good heart, and bear fruit with patience' (Luke 8:15)? What is the depth of their understanding and spiritual commitment? Whenever I read reports that speak in glowing terms of the success of a particular evangelistic campaign, and that state that so many hundreds of people made professions of Christian faith, I often think to myself, 'How many of these folk will still be going on with the Lord in twenty years' time?'

What is your response to the Lord Jesus Christ? Will it stand the test of time, or is it just a surface reaction that will eventually fade away with changing circumstances? Even if we are committed Christians, we can so often become excited after hearing a good sermon or reading a challenging Christian book, yet within the week we have forgotten all about it. The 'proof of the pudding' is not in that initial joy and thrill, but in whether there is any deep and lasting effect in our lives. Let us heed the warning of Ahab in this passage and beware of superficial emotions when we hear the Word of God.

Chapter 16

The wages of sin is death

(2 Kings 1)

We read in 2 Kings 1:1 that, after the death of Ahab, Moab rebelled against Israel. This national calamity was followed by a personal disaster, because Ahab's son Ahaziah, who succeeded him to the throne, fell out of a window and became very ill (v. 2). As a consequence, he sent messengers to inquire of Baal-zebub, god of Ekron, as to whether he would recover from this sickness. Notice that he didn't consult the Lord, the true God of Israel. He went instead to a heathen deity. However, as the messengers proceeded on their way, they were suddenly confronted by the prophet Elijah, who proclaimed a message from the Lord, namely, that Ahaziah's sickness was going to be fatal (v. 4). When the king heard about this (v. 6), he sent three groups of soldiers to the prophet Elijah. The captain of the first group went up to Elijah, who was sitting on the top of a hill, and said to him, 'O man of God, the king says, "Come down"' (v. 9). Elijah replied, 'If I am a man of God, let fire come down from heaven and consume you and your fifty [men]' (v. 10). Fire then came down from heaven and consumed them.

This raises the massive question: What on earth had these men done to deserve such a terrible judgement? The explanation which makes most sense is that these soldiers were guilty of gross insolence and, indeed, even blasphemy. Here they were, ambassadors of a king who didn't want to have anything to do with the true God of Israel, yet they had the effrontery to say to Elijah, 'O man of God, the king says, "Come down."' They were using the phrase 'man of God' to mock the prophet; this was an insult not merely to Elijah, but also to God himself, because the prophet was God's mouthpiece.

As a result, Elijah threw their words back at them, saying, in effect, 'If indeed I am what you mockingly say I am, let fire come down from heaven and consume you.' Let us remember that this was God's fire, not Elijah's. We might be tempted to think that Elijah was a hard-hearted man; however, if it hadn't been the Lord's will to send fire, there would have been no fire. Elijah was simply verbalizing what he discerned to be the will of God.

We might suppose that Ahaziah would have learnt his lesson after this. Not a bit! He sent out a second band of soldiers with the same impudence, indeed, even more so, because the message this time was 'Come down quickly!' (v. 11), as if to say, 'Hurry up, Elijah; we can't wait around for ever!' The result, though, was just the same: fire came down from heaven and consumed them.

Then came the third band of soldiers (v. 13). This time, instead of coming with a taunting, mocking attitude, the captain came with a spirit of respect for the prophet. He fell on his knees before Elijah in an attitude of humility and seeking mercy. In response, Elijah, as the mouthpiece of God, was only too willing to show mercy. The angel of the Lord said to Elijah, 'Go down with him; do not be afraid' (v. 15). The prophet then went down the hill to meet the king but didn't mince his words. He delivered a sober message of judgement (v. 16), which was fulfilled: the king 'died according to the word of the LORD that Elijah had spoken' (v. 17).

The restoration of Elijah to his old self

Before we consider the actual message delivered by the prophet in this passage, it is worth commenting on the attitude of Elijah himself. As with the case of Naboth's vineyard, here we have an example of Elijah having been restored to his old self. The Elijah of this chapter is once again the pre-wilderness, pre-broom tree prophet. Remember what kind of a man he was before his great depression. He was always on the front foot; he had stood boldly in the presence of Ahab, delivering an unpalatable message of judgement; he had confronted the Baal prophets on Mount Carmel, informing them that the party was over. He was utterly fearless. And as then, so now. He marched into the presence of the king and said, '... you shall not come down from the bed to which you have gone up, but you shall surely die.' This is the old Elijah who has been well and truly restored to the place where he can be a mighty tool in the hands of God.

This is surely a great encouragement to us as Christians today. Rarely are we in a state in which we can't think of better days. As we look back, we recall those periods when our love for the Lord Jesus Christ burned in our hearts and zeal for his kingdom was a living reality, whereas now we may feel much more like sitting down with Elijah under his broom tree. How comforting, therefore, to read about God restoring his children to spiritual vigour after a period of decline! Once again, Elijah is trusting in the promises of God. So, when the angel says, 'do not be afraid', we read that the prophet went off straight away to meet the king (v. 15). 'Don't be afraid,' says the Lord, 'I am with you. The king can't do you any harm. Look what I did to those soldiers who were out to destroy you: I consumed them with fire. I could do the same to the king if he stands in my way.'

If you are reading these words and are bowed down and discouraged, remember that Elijah's God is our God today. Cling on to the promises of God's protection and his presence with us at all times. Like Elijah, we need not be afraid of men, even kings, because we live in the presence of One who is the King of kings and Lord of lords. He has said, 'I am with you always, to the end of the age' (Matthew 28:20) and 'My grace is sufficient for you, for my power is made perfect in weakness' (2 Corinthians 12:9). God longs for us to lay hold of his precious promises and trust that he will be to us what he was to Elijah.

Elijah's message: the jealousy of God

Let us now look at the message which the prophet delivered. We find it recorded in verses 3 and 4, and then again in verse 16. Because Ahaziah decided to consult a heathen deity instead of the Lord God of Israel, he would die. God was consumed with a jealousy for his own position in the sight of the king and the nation. He wants to be given first place in the hearts and affections of his people, and, like a husband, he is jealous when the one whom he loves is unfaithful to him.

Is this notion of the jealousy of God merely an Old Testament idea? Not at all. In Revelation 2:4–5 we read the complaint of a jealous lover when the Lord Jesus Christ says to the church at Ephesus, 'I have this against you, that you have abandoned the love you had at first. Remember therefore from where you have fallen; repent, and do the works you did at first. If not, I will come to you and remove your lampstand from its place.'

There is a real sense in which God's heart burns for us with a holy jealousy today. He created us in order that we might give to him the love and devotion of our hearts. Why are we running after our Baal-zebubs? Why are we dabbling in areas of heathenism, pandering to the desires of the flesh? God is jealous for the undivided affection of our hearts. We may not, like Ahaziah, have sent someone on a trip to consult a pagan deity, but where do we go when it comes to setting the standards of our home lives? Do we go to the Word of God and govern our homes by the light of Scripture, or do we go to the latest pronouncements of non-Christian psychologists? When we allow other gods to dictate our home lives—husband–wife relationships, parent–child relationships, attitudes to Sunday worship and so on—then, in some measure, we are guilty of what Ahaziah was doing; we are going to a Baal-zebub for answers.

What about moral standards? Today in the UK, we can walk into any respectable newsagent's and pick up a handful of pornographic magazines. This would have been unthinkable just fifty years ago. It used to be regarded as a disgrace if two people lived together before they were married. Now it is regarded as the intelligent and sensible thing to do. Is our moral and ethical conduct to be governed by a modern-day Baal-zebub, or by the God of the Bible? We should surely be saying, 'I don't care what the sociologists or psychologists tell me; my God has said these are the standards which are to govern my life, and I'm prepared to die for them, if necessary.'

When it comes to education, we need to make sure that our children are not being taught by a Baal-zebub. When it comes to church life, we should not go to a Baal-zebub and ask him what works in the field of entertainment. We should go to the Lord and ask, 'What does your Word teach us about worship, prayer, preaching, giving and evangelism?' There is no need for the church to go running after the wisdom of the world. All that we need to know for our faith and practice is contained in the Bible. The Scriptures are an all-sufficient revelation (2 Timothy 3:16–17). It is tempting to go to the 'experts' for answers rather than consult the Scriptures; however, if the 'experts' don't speak from the Word of God, we should disregard them, even if they are wearing clerical collars! It is tragic that many Christian ministers today have substituted Baal-zebub for the plain teaching of

Holy Scripture. They have sold out to unbiblical, humanistic philosophy. And we wonder why God is not bringing reformation and revival to his church! If we go looking for answers from Baal-zebub, the result will be death and judgement, just as it was for King Ahaziah.

Our God burns with holy jealously for his church. We should therefore live and act as those who depend upon him as the only source of truth. 'Is it because there is no God in Israel that you are going to enquire of Baal-zebub?' (v. 3).

Chapter 17

The importance of dying well

(2 Kings 2:1–12)

In this chapter of 2 Kings we are treated to the final scene of the prophet's life on earth, before he was taken up to heaven. In verse 1 we read, 'Now when the LORD was about to take Elijah up to heaven by a whirlwind ...' The word 'when' denotes time, and the preposition 'by' indicates manner; according to this verse, the Lord is sovereign in both these areas. The time and the manner of Elijah's departure were in the hands of Almighty God. The same is true for us today. God is sovereign in choosing the time and the manner of our departure from this world.

The Lord will take the vast majority of Christians to himself by means of physical death. We will die and then we will find ourselves immediately in the presence of God. Jesus said to the dying thief on the cross, 'Truly, I say to you, today you will be with me in Paradise' (Luke 23:43). Of course, those who are alive when the Lord Jesus returns at the end of time will by-pass death. As Paul says in 1 Thessalonians 4:17, 'we who are alive, who are left, will be caught up together with them in the clouds to meet the Lord in the air, and so we will always be with the Lord.'

There were two people in the Old Testament who also by-passed death. One was Elijah, who, as we read in our chapter, was taken straight up into heaven by means of a whirlwind. The other man was Enoch, about whom we read, 'Enoch walked with God, and he was not, for God took him' (Genesis 5:24). Why did the Lord plan that both Enoch and Elijah should by-pass the normal processes of death? The Bible doesn't tell us. All we can do is echo the words of Jesus in Matthew 11:26: '... yes, Father, for such was your gracious will'. The Lord is absolutely sovereign in this, as in all other areas of life.

This truth has some important practical implications.

We should be ready to go at the Lord's bidding

Firstly, we should be prepared to go at the Lord's bidding. This was certainly true for Elijah. He knew that his time had come, so he said to Elisha, 'Ask what I shall do for you, before I am taken from you' (v. 9). Some people, like Elijah, know that their time has come. They can feel the spring of life beginning to wind down, and they know that their days are numbered. This is by no means always the case. For many, death will come suddenly and very unexpectedly. However, whether or not we are given any indications of our approaching death, it behoves all of us, like Elijah, to be prepared to go at the Lord's bidding.

We must accept the Lord's will regarding our loved ones

Secondly, it behoves us to accept the Lord's will in respect of our loved ones. There is some indication in our passage that Elisha had learnt this particular lesson. He accepted the fact that the Lord was going to take Elijah home, and so he said to the sons of the prophets in verse 3, 'Yes, I know it; keep quiet.'

Death is a great test for Christians, with regard both to themselves and to those to whom they are most closely attached, who may suddenly be snatched away at what seems an inopportune time and in ways that are beyond our understanding. Many Christians who have stood the test of persecution, opposition and many other onslaughts from the devil discover that their faith breaks down when faced with the death of loved ones. Do we really believe that God has the right to exercise this particular prerogative—to take one of his servants into heaven at the time and in the manner of his choosing? Can we say with Job, 'The LORD gave, and the LORD has taken away; blessed be the name of the LORD' (Job 1:21)?

One of the wonderful things about this passage is the picture it gives of Elijah's vigorous spirituality, even in the last hours before his departure from this world. This can be seen in at least three ways.

His strong faith

Firstly, notice his strong faith in verse 8. Elijah and his successor go down to the river Jordan in order to cross to the other side. However, Jordan is a large, formidable river, with rushing currents. So what does the prophet do? He simply pulls off his cloak, rolls it up and strikes the water—and the water parts for the two of them to walk across on dry ground! We may read this without thinking too much about it, but remember the elaborate preparations made for this very same miracle when God was bringing his people into the promised land under the ministry of Joshua (Joshua 3). For three days and nights, they waited by the banks of the river. On the day they were to pass across, the ark had to go in front at a certain specified distance. When the priests carrying the ark came to the edge of the waters, they had to stand still, and it was not until the priests' feet were covered to the ankles that God chose to part the waters. There was an elaborate religious ritual before this great event. Here, on the other hand, Elijah saunters up to the river, takes his cloak off, strikes the waters, and the two prophets cross over. What is this, if it is not a great picture of the strength of Elijah's faith right up to the very hour when he was ushered into the presence of God?

In Hebrews 11:1 we are told that 'faith is the assurance of things hoped for, the conviction of things not seen'. This being so, it ought to be the case that our faith deepens and grows as the prospect of eternal glory draws closer. Sadly, this is not always true for the people of God, but it certainly was true for Elijah. He had not become soured and jaundiced by the events of life, even though he had seen enough to jaundice most folk. He had seen a nation fall on its knees, crying, 'The LORD, he is God; the LORD, he is God', and yet, within a very short time, that same nation had returned to Baal worship. He had seen the unbelief and hostility of Ahab and his successor. He had seen enough to make a man ask, 'Is anything real?' However, in the last hour of his life, we have the evidence of a man of strong and vibrant faith.

A commendable humility

Secondly, we have the record of what seems to be a commendable humility. God had obviously indicated to Elijah that he was going to take him home to heaven in an unusual way, but the prophet wanted to be alone. He says to Elisha in verse 4, '… please stay here, for the LORD has sent me to Jericho.' Elisha insists upon going with him, but again in verse 6, Elijah says, 'Please stay here, for the LORD has sent me to the Jordan.' God is going to do a unique thing for Elijah, yet the prophet wants this great honour and privilege to be conducted in secret. God is going to send chariots and horses and take him straight up to heaven in a whirlwind, but Elijah doesn't want anyone else to be around to see it, not even Elisha. What a contrast to so many Christians, who, in their last days on earth, are doing all they can to bolster up their status and their reputation, doing anything to convince people that they are not 'has-beens'! Not so Elijah. He simply wants to fade out. He doesn't want his departure to be a great public spectacle. 'Leave me alone,' he says.

A great confidence in God's salvation

Thirdly, Elijah displays a great confidence in God's eternal salvation. Here is a man who knows that, within a very short space of time, he is going to be entering the presence of a God of blazing holiness; but there is no indication that he has any fear or anxiety about the prospect. Why was this? Surely it was because, by the operation of the Holy Spirit, he had been brought to a position of absolute confidence in what God had revealed about the reality of eternal glory. He knew that a world of eternal and spiritual reality exists beyond this world, so he wasn't afraid to depart this life. It is a great principle that, as our faith in the next world becomes the dominating factor in our lives, so we will live more effectively in this world. Isn't this what Paul is urging upon us at the beginning of Colossians 3? 'Set your minds', he says, 'on things that are above, where Christ is seated at the right hand of God' (see vv. 1–2). Christians can never think about heaven too much. The old adage says that we can be so heavenly minded that we are no earthly good, but the Bible teaches the opposite: the more heavenly minded we are, the more earthly good we shall be. May God grant that, like the prophet Elijah, we shall be so conversant with the world of eternity that, when the time comes for us to step out of this world into the next, it won't be too much of a shock to us, because we have been living there by faith already.

How often do we read Revelation 21–22? How often do we consider what it will be like to join Elijah, contemplating the face of the One who died for our sins on the cross? One of the marks of the great saints of God is that they are so familiar with the things of eternity that, to them, death is just like going out of the back door into the garden, leaving one sphere and stepping into another.

So here we have the picture of a man who, in the last hours of his life on earth, was in full bloom spiritually speaking—strong in his faith, genuine in his humility and unafraid to meet his Maker, because of his confidence in God's eternal salvation. One of the saddest things to see is a Christian who has lost his or her bloom, like plants in the garden at the end of summer—no longer lush, green and fertile, but brown, dry and straggly. There is no need to be like this. Listen to one of the great and encouraging promises which God has made to his people:

> The righteous flourish like the palm tree,
> and grow like a cedar in Lebanon.
> They are planted in the house of the LORD;
> they flourish in the courts of our God.
> They still bear fruit in old age;
> they are ever full of sap and green;
> to declare that the LORD is upright;
> he is my rock, and there is no unrighteousness in him.
> (Psalm 92:12–15)

What is the purpose of maintaining greenness and vitality? '[T]o declare that the LORD is upright; he is my rock, and there is no unrighteousness in him' (v. 15). In other words, our greenness is a witness to the character of God and the greatness of his salvation. How we need to pray that God would make us into such people. 'Lord, don't let me outlive the period of greenness. Lord, cut me off if otherwise I am going to wither and become a reproach to your holy name.' May ours be the experience of Elijah as we approach the time of our homecoming.

Chapter 18

The key to spiritual power

(2 Kings 2:9–14)

The secret of a powerful ministry

In this final chapter we will study the very last conversation between Elijah and Elisha, held just before Elijah was taken up to heaven in a whirlwind and chariots of fire. We read in verse 9 that, after they had crossed the Jordan, Elijah said to Elisha, 'Ask what I shall do for you, before I am taken from you.' Elijah was assuming the role of a father to a son and, in effect, saying to his successor, 'What do you want from me as a parting gift? You've lived with me for about six years. You've seen what it means to be the prophet of God in the midst of apostasy. What do you regard as the one indispensable thing that you need to equip you for the ministry that lies ahead?'

Elisha replies in verse 10, 'Please let there be a double portion of your spirit on me.' In other words, he wanted double the measure of spiritual power that had rested upon Elijah to rest upon him. After all, he was about to take Elijah's place on the stage of Israel. He was to be the mouthpiece of God to the nation—a nation that was still, for the most part, given over to the worship of Baal. Sad to relate, Elijah had not witnessed a genuine spiritual revival under his ministry. So Elisha was saying, 'If this is what happened under your ministry, Elijah, with the measure of the Spirit that you have known, then I surely need a double portion of that Spirit.'

This demonstrates Elisha's great insight into the secret of a powerful ministry. Such power is not to be found primarily in gifts and natural abilities, nor in training and human personality. Rather, it is to be found in the anointing of God the Holy Spirit. '[A]part from me you can do nothing,' said Jesus in John 15:5. We can have the gifts of eloquence and oratory; we can have most attractive natural personalities; however, unless the Spirit of God rests upon us, we will do nothing of eternal value. Elisha realized this, and that is why he said what he did.

Elisha's words reveal a deep humility. Some have suggested the very opposite. They say, 'Doesn't this request show pride? Who does Elisha think he is, asking for a double share of Elijah's spirit?' In actual fact, his request reveals his sense of total inadequacy for the task that lay ahead. It is as if Elisha is saying to his great forerunner, 'I'm so much less of a man than you are, Elijah; so if I'm ever to fill your shoes, I need twice the amount of spiritual power that you had.' That shows humility, not pride. The measure of true humility is the extent to which we realize, like Elisha, that we need the enabling power of the Holy Spirit in our lives. Are we continually crying to God that he would fill us with his Spirit because we realize that, left to our ourselves, we are just not competent to do what God requires of us? How often are we to be found in the place of prayer, beseeching God for ever-increasing supplies of his Spirit? One of the surest evidences of a proud heart is not so much someone puffing out his chest and saying, 'Look at me! What a great person I am!' Rather, it is failure to spend time with the Lord in prayer. The man or woman who neglects to pray is basically saying, 'I don't need God's help. I can cope quite well on my own, thank you very much.' To what extent do we find our hearts going out to the Lord in prayer, throughout the day, whenever we are in a situation of need? 'O Lord, help; O Lord, strengthen; O Lord, enable. I'm not adequate for this situation, in myself. I need your enabling grace to support me.' Is that your experience? Or do you think that you can do it all on your own?

A housewife, for example, might respond, 'Well, I'm not called to be a prophet as Elisha was. Certainly, if God told me that I was going to take Elijah's place, then I would ask the Lord to fill me daily with his Spirit—but I'm just a housewife!' But think for a moment of the vast implications of being a housewife and mother—the privilege of moulding and shaping the character of a future mother, a future father, a future citizen in the kingdom of Christ; and of being the instrument that encourages a husband in the direction of God and his will (the opposite would be subtly to dampen his spiritual desire and enthusiasm). What a vital role this is in the grand scheme of things! Someone else might say, 'I'm just a machine operator', or 'I'm just a librarian's assistant. My job is insignificant in the work of the gospel.' But the Bible makes it crystal clear that, whatever roles we fill, if we are Christians whose souls have been purchased by the blood of Christ, God has called us to be salt and light in those little circles of our world, however insignificant we may think they are; and we are no more adequate for that in our own strength than was Elisha for the work to which God had called him. We therefore *all* need to pray, 'Lord, fill me with the power of your Spirit, and so enable me to serve you in the situation in which you have placed me.'

What was Elijah's response to Elisha's request? We find it in verse 10: 'You have asked a hard thing; yet, if you see me as I am being taken from you, it shall be so for you, but if you do not see me, it shall not be so.' What is Elijah talking about here? I believe that he is indicating two very important principles.

Elisha needs to seek the blessing from God

Firstly, he is saying that Elisha needs to seek this blessing from God alone. He is saying, in effect, 'Elisha, whether you see me as I am being taken from you is something over which I have no control. I can't control the events of my departure from this world. But if the God who is about to take me so orders those events that you are allowed to see me as I go, then you'll have the blessing. God alone is in control, and he alone can give you the blessing you seek. You have asked a hard thing—so hard that I can't give it to you, but God can.'

What a vital principle for us to grasp today! If we want to live lives of spiritual power and grace, we must seek these things from God alone. 'Ask, and it will be given to you; seek, and you will find; knock, and it will be opened to you' (Matthew 7:7). If we really want to be men and women of God—if we want to know God in a deep way—we must persevere in prayer for these things. We must hunger and thirst for righteousness, and then we shall be satisfied. This doesn't mean that we are satisfied once and for ever; on the contrary, we have to go on hungering and thirsting. We need to go on realizing our perpetual need of God and all that he has to give us. Why do we not experience all the spiritual blessings which are promised to us in the Bible? It is because we have failed to plead with God to give them to us. He alone can do so.

Elisha needs to fix his eyes on eternity

The second principle Elijah wants to convey to his successor is this: 'Elisha, if your spiritual eyes are open to that heavenly world that exists beyond this world, then you'll have the blessing you desire. If you want a life and a ministry of spiritual power, your eyes need to be fixed upon the things of eternity, because one is a direct consequence of the other.' As we saw in the previous chapter, it is only as we fix our gaze upon heavenly realities that we will live lives of spiritual power and grace in this world. '[I]f you see me ... it shall be so for you.' If we want such lives it will be at the price of dealing mercilessly with anything that tends to dim our vision of heaven—those little specks that make our spiritual eyes insensitive to the things of God. I'm not talking about clear-cut sin but the area of doubtful things—the grey areas: things that we can rationalize as being legitimate for Christians that, if we are honest, cloud our spiritual vision. May God grant that our eyes would be open to that other world, so that we experience the power of Christ in this world.

When we speak to our non-Christian friends about spiritual matters, is there a hollow ring of unreality about what we say? Or do we speak with a depth of real conviction because we are speaking about a world of eternal reality with which we are familiar? Do our friends realize that we not just playing with words and religious ideas, but, as we speak and live before them, in a very real sense we are giving them a taster of the powers of the world to come? '[I]f you see me ... it shall be so for you.'

God graciously answered this request of Elisha's; we read in verse 12 that he was privileged to see his great father in the faith go up into heaven, and he cried out, 'My father, my father! The chariots of Israel and its horsemen!' and he saw him no more. Then, as a direct consequence of this heavenly vision, he received the spiritual power for which he had asked; we read in verses 13–14 that he went back to the Jordan, took Elijah's cloak and struck the water, saying, 'Where is the LORD, the God of Elijah?' Then the water was parted and he went across. In this way, God confirmed to his servant Elisha that he had indeed equipped him for the work to which he had been called: firstly, by allowing him to take up the cloak that belonged to Elijah; and secondly, by enabling him to perform precisely the same miracle as his predecessor had done only a few moments before. Elisha was now able to embark upon his ministry in the confidence that he went forward, not in his own strength, but in the strength and the power of the spirit of Elijah.

As we come to the end of these studies, we need to pray as individuals and as churches that the Lord God of Elijah would fill us all with the power of his Spirit, so that we might see truth and righteousness established in our own hearts and then, overflowing from that, in the hearts and lives of those around us. May God grant that in our generation we might see the Lord so breathe upon his church in revival power that the world would be confronted, not only with the glorious message of salvation, but also with the reality and the effect of that message, as people see us living in vital contact with the world of eternity.

This final scene began with Elijah's successor acknowledging his own helplessness. I trust that at this point we feel at one with Elisha. As we face the task of seeking to confront a world of apostasy with the good news of the gospel, may we be constrained to cry to God, 'Lord, we can't do this ourselves. We need your power and your strength to help us. Give us daily an increasing measure of your Holy Spirit!' May that be the burden of our prayers as we seek to be Christ's witnesses in today's world.

About Day One:

Day One's threefold commitment:

- TO BE FAITHFUL TO THE BIBLE, GOD'S INERRANT, INFALLIBLE WORD;
- TO BE RELEVANT TO OUR MODERN GENERATION;
- TO BE EXCELLENT IN OUR PUBLICATION STANDARDS.

I continue to be thankful for the publications of Day One. They are biblical; they have sound theology; and they are relative to the issues at hand. The material is condensed and manageable while, at the same time, being complete—a challenging balance to find. We are happy in our ministry to make use of these excellent publications.

JOHN MACARTHUR, PASTOR-TEACHER, GRACE COMMUNITY CHURCH, CALIFORNIA

It is a great encouragement to see Day One making such excellent progress. Their publications are always biblical, accessible and attractively produced, with no compromise on quality. Long may their progress continue and increase!

JOHN BLANCHARD, AUTHOR, EVANGELIST AND APOLOGIST

Visit our website for more information and to request a free catalogue of our books.

www.dayone.co.uk

www.dayonebookstore.com

Saul and Sons
Decline and fallout in the family of Israel's first king

BRIAN H EDWARDS

ISBN 978–1–84625–226–6

128PP PAPERBACK

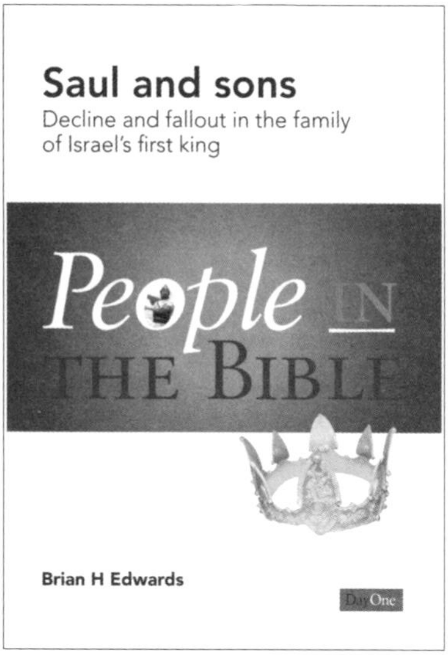

Israel's first king began with great promise and ended in tragedy. The author traces Saul's head start into the monarchy and the accelerating spiral into possibly the most lamentable biography in the Bible. Along the way there is much to learn from a king whose story is told in Scripture so that we might understand the ways of a man who fell out with God and fell in with the powers of darkness. There are surprises along the way, not least in the story of his son who, but for the purposes of God, would surely have made an excellent king. However, on the blood-spattered walls of Beth Shan, the story does not quite end. There is another member of Saul's line who shines with bright hope and reflects the character of his godly father in contrast to that of his tragic grandfather.

An accessible book for every reader which, as well as bringing the three characters of Saul, Jonathan and Mephibosheth to life and clarifying difficulties in the text, concludes every chapter with questions for thoughtful discussion suitable for group or personal study.

Brian Edwards gained his theological degree from the University of London before entering the pastoral ministry for the next thirty years. He then took on a wider role of preaching and lecturing both in the UK and abroad. Brian has authored or co-authored more than twenty books on theological, historical and biographical subjects. He and his wife Barbara, who died in 1998, prepared the widely used marriage preparation course published under the title *No Longer Two*. He also edits the popular Travel Guide series published by Day One and is chairman of the Editorial Board of the *Praise!* hymnbook.

Brian lives in Surrey, England and has two sons and three granddaughters.

People in the Bible: Barnabas: A good man, full of faith

ROBERT DALE

ISBN 978–1–84625–088–0

128PP PAPERBACK

If Christians were to vote for their favourite Bible character, Barnabas would surely be in the top ten. Most of us feel drawn to this warm-hearted disciple, who so wonderfully lives up to his name, 'Son of Encouragement'. In these character studies based on passages in Acts, Robert Dale helps us to appreciate—and encourages us to imitate—this wonderful man, who himself is a reflection of a still greater Man, our Lord Jesus Christ, the greatest Encourager of all.

Robert Dale is pastor of Lincoln Evangelical Church, in the East of England. Converted at the age of twenty-two, he worked for seventeen years in the City of London, before becoming pastor of a small Baptist church in Surrey in 1988; he moved to Lincoln in 2002. He and his wife, Jane, have a son, Jonathan, and a daughter, Hannah.

'This is a very uplifting book. Here you will find copious investigation, studious exposition and judicious application from the Biblical record of a generous man so full of Christ that he was a constant encouragement to the church. What more could you ask for?'
John Benton, editor, **Evangelicals Now,** ***and author***

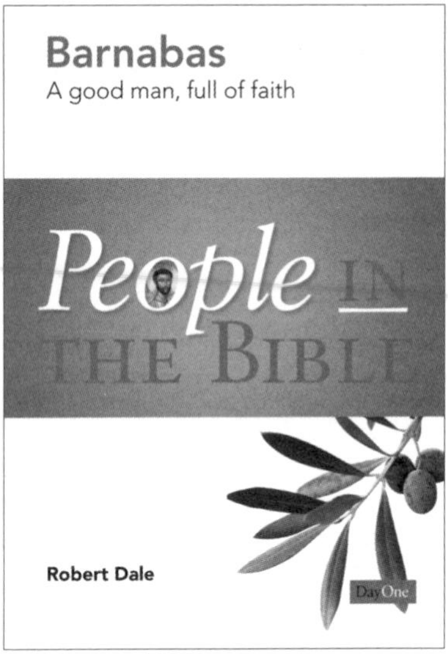

'It is easy to underestimate the apostle Barnabas, who is overshadowed by his fellow worker, the apostle Paul. Robert Dale's study displays Barnabas' godly character, increases our appreciation of his role in the growth of the New Testament church, and draws numerous insights of application for personal godliness and the work of the ministry. Recommended for pastors and lay readers.'
Les Bollinger, Pastor, Beaver Baptist Church, Beaver, Pennsylvania

People in the Bible—Samson
Man of strength, man of weakness

COLIN D JONES

ISBN 978–1–84625–089–7

96PP PAPERBACK

The story of Samson is one of the most exciting and intriguing in the whole of Scripture. As the sub-title suggests, it is a simultaneous insight into his incredible strength and persistent weakness. We marvel at the thrilling accounts of unorthodox battles and awe inspiring demonstrations of physical power. Sadly, we also wonder at his apparent inability to learn from his own mistakes as he follows his passions to their inevitable end. This rollercoaster of a story sweeps us from the rich promises accompanying his birth, though the tragedies and triumphs of his life. The story almost ends with the pitiable sight of him as the blind captive of his life-long enemies the Philistines. Yet, there is still one surprising twist to this epic tale—victory through death. Throughout we trace the contrasts with the great Judge of Israel—Christ.

Colin D Jones has been in the ministry since 1971. He became the pastor of Three Bridges Free Church, Crawley in 1996 after twenty-two years of ministry at Wem Baptist Church, Shropshire. He is a long serving member of the Council of the FIEC and is author of *Exploring Esther: Serving the unseen God*, also published by Day One. He and his wife, Chris, have four daughters: Esther, Abigail, Tirzah and Miriam.

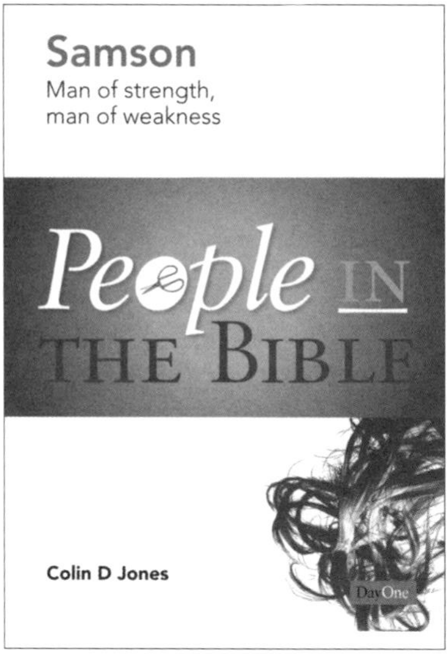

Read this work for profit and praise, for a greater than Samson has come into the world.

Clive Anderson, Pastor of 'The Butts' Church, Alton, Hampshire, England

'Colin Jones has made an enigmatic narrative powerfully relevant. This is the story of Samson—for today. Careful exegesis, confronting the hard parts with honesty, and comparing and contrasting with the life of Jesus Christ, together with practical application, makes this commentary a powerful blend of personal Bible Study aid, a group discussion starter and a challenge for every Christian life. An accessible must for anyone interested in the life and times of Samson and its relevance for today.'

Brian H Edwards

God's Little People

A TRILOGY FROM BRIAN H EDWARDS LOOKING AT SOME OF THE LESSER-KNOWN PEOPLE WHOSE LIVES MADE A DIFFERENCE

For every person whose name blazes across the pages of our heritage of history in the large letters of a Tyndale, Bunyan, Wesley, Spurgeon or Lloyd-Jones, there are tens of thousands of 'little people' who have courageously and faithfully maintained a stand for the truth and have extended the borders of the Kingdom of God. It is upon these that the Lord builds his church. Fascinating insights from Brian H Edwards in these volumes. Scripture index included in each.

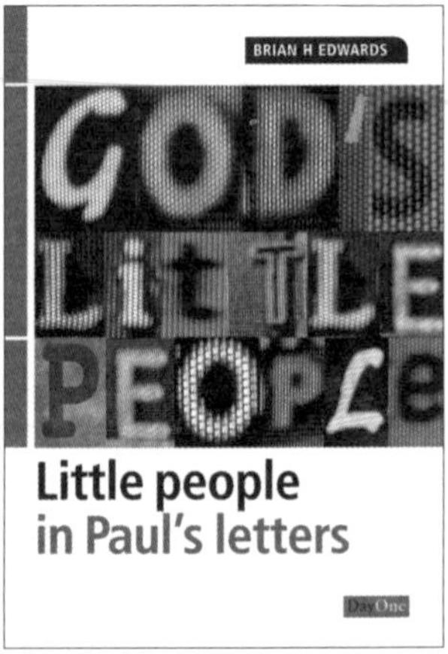

GOD'S LITTLE PEOPLE: LITTLE PEOPLE IN PAUL'S LETTERS, ISBN 978–1–903087–85–5

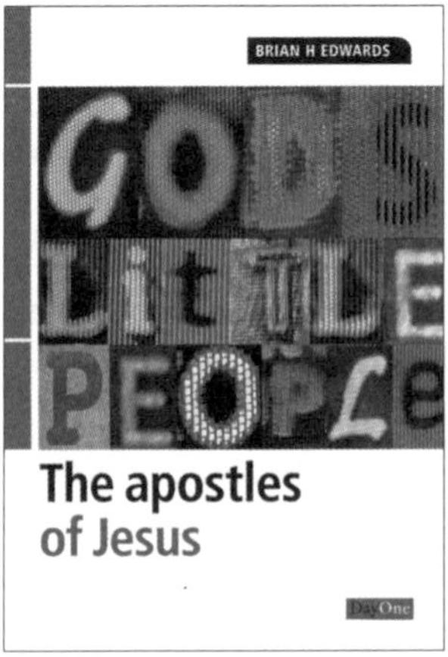

GOD'S LITTLE PEOPLE: THE APOSTLES OF JESUS, ISBN 978–1–903087–94–7

GOD'S LITTLE PEOPLE: LITTLE WOMEN IN THE BIBLE, ISBN 978–1–84625–025–5